I0486971

HOW TO BECOME A SUCCESSFUL ENTREPRENEUR

AND

HOW TO MAKE BAD GUYS FINISH LAST

I

HOW TO BECOME A SUCCESSFUL ENTREPRENEUR

PREFACE

This book, *How to Become a Successful Entrepreneur,* subtitled *How to Make Bad Guys Finish Last* is a deceptively easy-read.

The author brings to the reader, details of where, when, and how to bring forth your new venture. You will see why timing is so important, why a *market niche is everything.*

For you, the entrepreneur who is struggling or about to embark on the new venture, there is herein guidance in the best way to begin. For the business which has grown somewhat successfully, and faces cash-flow challenges due to that very growth, there are solutions with OPM.

And, for the already successful entrepreneur, (who has perhaps been able to set aside his or her initial *gelt*) and built an asset base of value, you will succeed in your *Exit Plan* by following the detailed recommendations to not let the *Bad Guy* in, and if he, like the parable of the camel in the tent from ancient story, somehow has managed to penetrate your assets, you will find ways to *Make the Bad Guys Finish Last!*

Gelt , through ongoing profits or by exit plan, is your retirement plan. You predicatably will have little medical insurance, no Pension or 401(k)

There are many, nearly a plethora, of writers on entrepreneurial themes. Many of these works are worthy of your readership. However, few of them have the author's background of hands-on experience in entrepreneurship.

By acquiring, creating, growing, and capitalizing more than a half-dozen manufacturing and other business entities, the author exceeded the entrepreneurial norm of "5 projects by age 55".

HOW TO MAKE BAD GUYS FINISH LAST

About the Author. Born in Salt Lake City, Utah. August 12, 1920, the author was reared in Columbus, and Oxford, Ohio, where his father, Harry James Russell taught Romance Languages, first at Ohio State then at Miami Universiy.

From a family of professionsals (only his grandfather bewas an entrepreneur), he was a mini-entrepreneur. At an early age, he spread black walnuts in the street, and passing cars removed the thick green outside finger-staining cover,

A graduate of Miami University, Oxford, Ohio, he became proficient in Spanish as a Mormon missionary in Argentina. He then served in a "cloak and dagger" capacity for the U.S. Army, G-2, M.I.S., during World War II, as Executive for Intelligence to the Military Attaches in the American Enbassies of Argentina, Brazil, and Costa Rica.

His first business experience was in San Francisco, California, in export and domestic sales. Here he met and married Dorothy Richardson from Manassa, Colorado and Salt Lake City. There followed a move to Puerto Rico, where for 21 years, Russell engaged in enentrepreneurial ventures: leveraged buyouts of floundering manufacturing companies; consulting services to dozens of others. And "turnkey" factory installations.

He continues to be a Business Advisor to the Synergy Companies in Californa, and Zion Foundation in Salt Lake City, Utah. He also serves as advisor to various universities and civic Boards of Directors and Trustees.

Warm weather and water lovers, the author and his wife Dorothy reside on the Main Canal on a barrier reef in Satellite Beach, Florida. It is a short trip by boat to their youngest daughter's dock and from there to their son's dock. They have 4 children, 14 grandchildren, and 7 great-grandchildren.

In this, his 88th year, Russell published a fact-based historical novel, *Timely Heroes,* subtitled *Under the Southern Cross,* available at *Amazon.com,* a true swashbucking tale of three naval Masters and Commanders, unsung American heroes who turned the tide of the revolution of the Spanish Colonies in Argentina, 1814.

DISCLAIMER

HOW TO MAKE BAD GUYS FINISH LAST

COPYRIGHT PAGE

Second Edition

Copyright © 1999/2008 Gardner H. Russell

Printed in the United States of America

Library of Congress Catalogue Card Number 98-96688

Russell, Gardner
  *How to Become a Successfuk Entrepreneur,/
  and how to make bad guys finish last./by
  Gardner H. Russell

  ISBN Number 1-4392-6176-8   SAN 299 7436
  1. New business enterprises--United States. 2.
  Entrepreneurship-United States. 3. Self-employed--
  United States. 4. Small business-United States. 1.
  Title.   10 9 8 7 6 5 4 3 **2** 1

  First Edition title: The Effective Entrepreneur -3999
  copies.

DEDICATION

To my wife Dorothy Annette Russell, for her ever willingness 'to go the extra mile' in proof-reading *How to Become a Successful Entrepreneur* and *How to Make Bad Guys Finish Last*. It is also dedicated to my mentor, U.S. Congressman Burton Lee French, and to Dr. Harry J. Russell, Ph.D., father, example, and author.

INTRODUCTION

How to Become a Successful Entrepreneur is dedicated to tens of thousands of entrepreneurs, *The Good Guys*. You may have aready embarked upon that new venture and are struggling at one level or another.

Or you may be a budding entrepreneur who has made the *Big Decision* and is actively planning that first business. Or you may be one of countless *"Entrepreneurial Wannabes"*, *Good Guys* , men and women who yearn to be in their own enterprises. No matter in which group you may be at present, you will find value in this book.

The author has included actual case studies, *"Illustration Capsules,"* interspersed with *"Rules,"* suggestions and recommenations, italicized for ready reference.

You may be a *Good Guy with Good Luck,"* or a "Good Guy with Bad Luck". In these pages you will learn how to become a successful *entrepreneur* with ways to improve your chances and protect yourself against *Bad Guys.*

A *Bad Guy* is defined for our purposes as *"Anyone who, by any means, seeks to take away the assets of Good Guys."*

The author is grateful for his many interesting experiences with hundreds of *Bad Guys,.* He has made many of them *Finish Last.* He has made an exhaustive study of these *Bad Guys* and their methods as they assiduously set about to attack and divest the *Good Guys* of their assets.

May you, the reader, one of the **Good Guys**, learn and apply the lessons of this volume to succeed in *Becoming a Successful Entrepreneur* There is joy in making *Bad Guys Finish Last.*

Good luck!

HOW TO BECOME A SUCCESSFUL ENTREPRENEUR

CONTENTS

HOW TO MAKE BAD GUYS FINISH LAST

HOW TO BECOME SUCCESSFUL ENTREPRENEUR

AND

HOW TO MAKE BAD GUYS FINISH LAST

SECOND (REVISED) EDITION

The Author also published *Timely Heroes,* subtitled *Under the Southern Cross,* It is a fact-based historical novel of derring-do of three Americans, *Masters and Commanders,* who created a naval squadron (1813-1814) in Buenos Aires, Argentina..

The squadron sailed out to do battle with, and soundly defeat, the Spanish Commander, who, with 30 warships, manning a total of 840 cannon, blockaded Montevideo

To My Reader

This is not a definitive work on *entrepreneurs and entrepreneurship*. I leave that to the Druckers, Mancusos and other Deans of Entrepreneurial Studies.

How To Become a Successful Entrepreneur may, however, be the best *How To* book in the entrepreneurial field today. As you embark on this read of verities of *How to Become a Successful Entrepreneur*, I suggest you fine-tune your ability to listen and thoughtfully consider. And, keep in mind two *Verities,*

> *They that will not be counselled, (i.e. do*
> *not listen) cannot be helped. If you do not*
> *hear reason, she'll rap you on the knuckles.*
> *Benajmin Franklin*
>
> *If we only begin, the mind becomes heated.*
> *Only be gin and the w ork i s c ompleted .*
> *Anonymous.*

Let's begin by considering how many common *Entrepreneurial Traits and Attributes* (facing page) you have, They are only a guide, not an absolute requirement for success,.

My only son, the entrepreneur, readied our filter factory for sale, and simultaneously processed meat packaging for the Latin American market. He has never been an avid book reader. Yet, he just completed his Exit Plan and retired. with a net worth nearly 10 times mine. Go figure!

Gardner Russell, Author
645 Cinnamon Court,
Satellite Beach, Florida 32937

Entrepreneurial Traits and Attributes

If you wish to become a successful entrepreneur, it might be advantageous to review the list below and determine what *attributes you already have*, and what attributes you may want to acquire. It would be a plus if you are:

- in an endless quest for knowledge in many areas
- unwilling or unable to work in structured public or private activity
- a constant reader of books and magazines (or equivalent - the author read 3 to 4 books a week for many years)
- a networker with anyone he or she meets
- able to identify and combine known technologies to create a new product or service
- able to identify market niches
- driven to succeed and willing to work hard
- a participant in business activities as a youth
- independent and confident
- able to make good common sense decisions
- be able to distill the essential from a mass of data
- quite personable and one who cares for people already (or becomes a *people-person)*
- of high self-esteem and self-confidence
- achievement, not money, driven
- able to view possible failures as a learning process toward eventual success
- certain that there are no problems, only challenges
- *rerum novarum cupidus* (driven to do new things)
- computer literate and at ease on the Internet
- endowed with *street smarts*
- able to think "outside the box", i.e. be creative
- proficient in basic financial matters

How to be a Successful Entrepreneur
is written for the most part in a narrative form, Entrepreneurial ***Illustration Capsules***, and ***Rules*** - many from the author's personal experiences- are included to give flavor and substance to the verities set forth herein.

Tens of thousands of individuals are entrepreneurial "wannabes' who are *constrained by obvious realities:* a built-in fear of change; the perceived security of a regular paycheck; or the corporate promise of job security and retirement. Their latent entrepreneurial spirit is anesthetized. If you are a would-be entrepreneur, you will find in this book proven ways to embark on your own successful entrepreneurial venture - and ways to thwart Bad Guys who lie in wait..

CHAPTER ONE

ENTREPRENEURS' FATAL DISTRACTIONS

The Rationale. Illustration Capsule One: The Distraction of Reaching for the Gold Ring in the Business Merry-Go-Round. Illustration Capsule Two: The Distraction of Perceived Infallibility, and llustration Capsule Three: The Fatal Distraction of the Greedy Associate.

Theater **he Rationale**

Early this year, my granddaughter's voice on the telephone was high-pitched with excitement. She had just returned from a visit to her sister.

"Grandaddy, a man on the plane was reading *your book*!"

This was remarkable because the *First Edition* of my book, *The Effective Entrepreneur*, subtitled, *How to Make Bad Guys Finish Last* (1999-2000) had been out of print for several years.

The Effective Entrepreneur enjoyed modest success. The first print-run of 3,000 books was published and sold out. My message to the entrepreneurial community was read by thousands.

One of three universities in which *The Effective Entrepreneur* was taught as a course placed an order several years ago for a substantial number of books. I had organized *Advantage Publishing Company* and 'did it all' (marketing, packing, shipping, billing etc).

Print-On-Demand technology was not yet available. As I contemplated the work involved, an apt phrase came to mind, which I learned from a wonderful friend, Elder Gene R. Cook, with whom I served as a full-time volunteer (General Authority - *Quorums of the Seventy 1986 to 1991*-of the *Church of Jesus Christ of Latter-day Saints* "Mormon"). I commend the phrase to you, **"Yes, I guess not!"**

For the past two years, I obsessed with the research and writing of a true story that I stumbled onto 40 years ago. It is a true historical novel, *Timely Heroes*, subtitled *Under the Southern Cross*, (*Booksurge Publishing* and *Amazon.com*) August 2008). It is a swashbuckling tale of three seafaring Americans, *Masters and Commanders*, whose lives came together in Buenos Aires, Argentina.

Along with a fearless Irishman, and a Visionary Rebel Leader, they turned the tide against Spain (1810-1814).

After sending *Timely Heroes* to my Publisher, (Booksurge Publishing) I considered the *Effective Entrepreneur* once again.,

As I prepared the Outline for a possible *Second Edition*, of the *Effecctive Entrepreneur*, I became excited. Yes, the intervening 8 years witnessed quantum leaps in valuable information and insight. With a revised *Second Edition*, I could better serve existing entrepreneurs: those starting their own businesses; and those on what I call *Their Ever-Inclining Plane* toward entrepreneurship. And those who have a burning desire to *be on their own* but are *constrained from doing so, because of obvious realities!* - such as the tendency to resist change, to remain in an unhappy employment situation. Should my message reach a few more men and women, that will be reward.enough. And so, welcome to the *Second Edition, How to Become a Successful Entrepreneur* subtitled *And How to Make Bad Guys Finish Last*

Note: All proceeds go to *The Gardner and Dorothy Russell Entrepreneurial Endowment Scholarship Funds at BYU Hawaii, BYU Idaho*, and *Southern Virginia University.Timely Heroes* (*Booksurge Publishing*) Available at Amazon.com

Illustration Capsule One ; The Distraction of Reach ing for the Gold Ring in the Business Merry-Go-Round

Joel (not his real name) has an excellent paying job with a Police Force. He has a special ability to get criminals to turn themselves in.

Joel was not apparently aware that by starting a new business of his own, *while he kept his day job,* he could build his *gelt.* He has a *good head for business.*

A few months ago I met with Joel. We discussed several ideas involving the manufacture of existing products, with innovations and added value. This is what entrepreneurs do best, *add value to an existing niche product.*

I was impressed with Joel's knowledge and product ideas. Several were superior to my own.

But, Joel has a *near-fatal distraction,* and is financially 'tapped-out'as a result. This same distraction has caused thousands of individuals, so intent on making the *Big Score,* to be prevented from becoming successful entrepreneurs. I call it a *Fatal Distraction, striving to catch the gold ring on the business Merry-go-round.*

Joel decided he could amass a fortune by investing in several medium to high risk businesses. He became a welcome OPM (Other Peoples' Money) source to three Companies.

One was a secondary oil recovery operation, sometimes a moderate-risk investment. Unfortunately, a very high sulphur content contaminated the recovered oil, too expensive to process. The substantial monthly payments ceased.

The second venture was and is high-risk, since the main product had not been properly field tested and did not work in production.

The third company has a process to convert *green waste* (trees, bushes, grass, etc.) to electricity. It is extremly high-risk, and due to problems beyond the Founder's control, has already diluted the first tier of investors.

The Promotor, a friend of Joel's, knew that Joel did not have substantial discretionary funds and yet, unconscionably, sold Joel on the idea that his investment would put him on what we used to call *Easy Street*.

This one is *Joel's baby* and he gets upset if anyone says anything critical of the baby. Joel asked me my opinion.

"Joel, I will match all the dividends you receive from your investment in the *green* company in the next five years!"

He was so far distracted that he thought that statement indicated my approval of the project. (I hope I have to *eat my words* and that he reaps a reward.)

It is almost impossible to catch the gold ring in the *Merry-Go-Round of risky Start-Ups or Good Ideas.*

> **Rule***: Don't be an OPM bird (a kind of 'pigeon') in a risky venture's nest. Use only discretionary funds for such investments, also known as 'throw-at-the-wall money, to see if something sticks!'*

> **Corollary***: Never invest your **gelt** in risky venturess ('gelt' includes savings. rainy-day monies, college funds, or other assets). Invest in nothing riskier than your 401K, Pension Plan, Income-Producing Real Estate, FDIC-Secured Certificates of Deposit, or a modest portion as seed money for that new enterprise.*

A word about heavy investments in the stock market. Invest carefully with a small portion of your gelt. Should you decide to seriously play the stock market, first try to think of a person you know who has all or most of his or her assets in the stock market, and is still wealthy as a result. *I never met one* in all my friends and acquaintances.

Illustration Capsule Two ;The Distraction of Perceived Infallibility - Manhattan Broom Company.

A gentleman by the name of Meckes came into my office. He was a big man, handsome, wealthy, proud of his German-Jewish heritage. After introductions, he said,

"Mr. Russell, my brother and I have supplied *Manhattan Broom Company* with more than $100,000 of fiber broom material from India. We fear that the Owner, Carlos Lozano, is not capable of operating the fiber broom business at a profit. He has indicated that he would be willing to sell the business. We are told that you can help us."

In response to my questions, he informed me that there was only one location in India where one could buy 5 ounce broom fiber bundles, hand-tied, of a special black fiber. It was available nowhere else in the world.

"The problem, Mr. Russell, is that the town where they process the fiberis close to the Chinese border. Every time there is an incursion by China's troops into India, the fiber supply dries up. For that reason we have to keep a large inventory of fiber bundles."

I visited the small factory, on a mountainside in Trujillo Alto, a suburb of San Juan, Puerto Rico. It was housed in a small, dark and gloomy building, with a hard-packed dirt floor. Its sole machine clanked away, stamping out identical metal parts for the broom case.

These parts were painted red and allowed to dry in a homemade oven. The small bundle of black fiber was then spread evenly on one side of the formed metal piece. The other piece was affixed and the broom handle inserted in what was now a metal case. After passing through a riveting machine, the fiber broom was finished.

I met the genial young Colombian who was sole owner of the broom company. He was always smiling and gracious, opened the financial records, such as they were. I had just enjoyed the exhilarating success of my Exit Plan in another business, in which I sold my interests for low six-figures, - income tax-free - to my former Associates.

I had become infallible (or so I thought) and could do no wrong. So, for the first and only time in my entrepreneurial life, I failed to do due diligence. I eyeballed the inventory, gave only a cursory look at the financial statements. After all, it was a very small, straightforward deal. And I took note that the independent accountant who had prepared the financials was well-regarded on the island.

And so, I negotiated the purchase. The total Purchase Price was $20,000, justified by the $23,000 Net Worth of Manhattan Broom. I was pleased, it was a Buy-Out at value of total assets.

And, in what I thought was another one of my brilliant ideas, I induced the Meckes to exchange Non-Voting, Low-Interest Preferred Stock for his $100,000 Account Payable, plus an Equity Kicker of one-third of the issued and outstanding shares of common stock of Manhattan Broom Company. The Balance Sheet now showed $123,500 Net Worth, since the Preferred Stock was considered to be Capital, not Debt.

I was managing two other compares at the time. Together with Manhattan Broom, they were the first growth equity investments of INSA, INC., in which I held a controlling interest.

To my dismay, the cash position, even after I brought in

past due Accounts Receivable, was extremely tight. I verified the inventory, then, belatedly, did my due diligence on the Financial Statements. The reality soon leaped out. My eyes widened. I thought

"Carlos, *bless your heart,* you posted the *total sales twice,* and the cost of sales only once!"

The net result was that Manhattan Broom Company, instead of a $23,000 Net Worth Company at the time of my acquisition, was in reality bankrupt-- with a *Minus* $20,000 Net Worth.

The Accountant had either been in *cahoots* with Carlos, or failed to review the numbers. The charming Colombian rogue was probably enjoying a *pisco sour* in Bogotá Columbia with his small windfall! In retrospect, I should probably have turned the Company over to the Meckes and taken the loss.

But, if I had, I would not have stored a wonderful memory. I get tender just recalling the experience. The woman next door to the broom factory, lived in a small, neat house that seemed to cling precariously to the mountainside. On the small porch,which overlooked the valley below, there was a tiny table and one chair.

She agreed to prepare exquisite *criollo* (native) lunches for me. After serving me, she discreetly disappeared. The mountainside undulated downward. (Nearly all the mountains in Puerto Rico are benign and friendly).

As I awaited my lunch, hummingbirds flitted with complete trust around me, sipped at the nectar from an arching honeysuckle vine. A profusion of flowers, flowering bushes and trees carpeted the gently sloping side of the mountain as it fell away to the valley.

Delicate, mixed fragrances wafted in on a light, but steady, breeze. It was a botanist's dream. Double red and yellow hibiscus trees, long-since matured from bushes, a blanket of periwinkle in many colors, the poisonous, but incredibly lovely, bright yellow flowers of the *Canario* (Canary) plant.

Here and there, standing straight and tall, with pods of red blooms perched upright at the end of each branch, were the *Emperatriz de la Selva* trees. (Empress of the Jungle - Tulip Trees). Interspersed were *Flamboyanes* (Flame Trees) which exploded into bright red blossoms in June and stayed beautiful for weeks. Never has scenery affected me more deeply. I could hardly wait for lunch each day!

As reality sank in, it was obvious that something had to be done to save Manhattan Broom. The market was narrow. A hnndful of Spaniards (first generation *Gallegos* from *Galicia*, Spain) controlled the Wholesale Fiber Broom market. And a competitor had just entered the market. His name was Tato Folch. We shared the market at $7.10 a dozen. I met with Tato and suggested he call on half the Spanish buyers and I the other half and that we keep prices steady. He agreed. A few days later   my Sales Manager came into my office, shaking his head,

"Señor Russell, I called on our customers like you said, but Tato had already been there, and sold them brooms!"

Tato was obviously not going to honor our Agreement.

I invented additions to the metal case forming machine. Soon, five operations were made by the machine and manufacturing costs sharply reduced. But so were the broom prices as Tato and I did battle - from $7.10 to $4.05 a dozen.

Then Tato offered to buy my stock in the broom company for $50,000. I asked my Associates, the Meckes, who had shown themselves capable of operating the broom business, what they would pay for my (INSA's) equity interest,

"Gardner, we think you ahould tranfer your interest at no cost to us. Afer all, we have had to build the fiber inventory to $200,000 to service increased sales."

"Gerhard, as you know, INSA has taken only $1,000 a month for General Management and Manhattan Broom now has a respectable Net Worth. Tato has offered to buy INSA's interest for middle five figures. I will sell the majority interest to you for $10,000." They finally agreed.

I was finally able to move on to better things. Never again was I to fail to do due diligeence, nor did I think I was infallible. This was indeed nearly a *Fatal Distraction*. I had nobody to blame but myself! How could I have embraced the *False Doctrine of Infallibilty*?

> **Rule**: *No entrepreneur, from the small*
> *est to the greatest can ever consider him*
> *or herself infallible. Do the necessary*
> *due diligence on every venture.*

I smile as I recall that, as an adjunct to the broom business, I started to manufacture *coladores*. A man came to my office with a a machine that formed wire into the handle and the circular loop of the frame of the *colador*.

At the time, Puerto Ricans steeped their coffee until it became almost an elixir. They strained out the grounds from the concentrated liquid, using the *colador*, which looked like a tiny butterfly net. The thick liquid was poured into a cup of hot milk and sugar added. This is the way coffee had been served for decades. It was a good business.

Soon there were dozens of women sewing the cloth into tiny flannel nets onto the wire frames and sales reached 2000 dozen coladores a month.

Then *Nestle* came to Puerto Rico with instant coffee. The

cultural change was, amazingly, almost immediate. The laborious process of rendering coffee into elixir, almost a century old, was replaced by *café instantáneo*. My Sales Manager came to me, wringing his hands.

"What can we do? *Coladores* aren't selling"

"Jorge, you'll just have to convince the women to pour their instant coffee through the wire frame, and we'll forget the little bag!"

I burst into laughter. He was not amused.

> **Rule:** Should a niche market collapse, for whatever reason, the entrepreneur must stand ready to immediately create, manufacture, and market other value-added products or services.

Illustration Capsule Three ; Distraction of the Greedy Associate: Electronic Manufacturing Engineers, Inc.

Though EME was profitable, it badly needed additional working capital.

A slight man, Sam Jones, from Connecticut-- skin bronzed from years of sailing--asked if he could invest in one of my ventures. He had inherited several million dollars. I suggested that he purchase 20% of the shares of common voting stock of *Electronic Manufacturing Engineers, Inc.,* and INSA, INC. would acquire 40%.

Electronic Manufacturing Engineers manufactured fractional horsepower motors under contract with United Airlines, toroidal coils (I was never quite sure what they were), resistors, etc.

Sam signed a letter to the effect that he would vote his shares of common voting stock with INSA's at all times. With Sam's equity interest, I controlled 60% of the common voting stock of EME. Hugh MacPherston and Ward Dabson, creators of EME, owned 20% each. Hugh was primarily a developer, an opportunist -- not overtly greedy or crooked.

Ward was as *crooked as a dog's hind leg*; a greedy, disbarred attorney who had fled San Francisco for a life in Puerto Rico. I thought I could handle him. Wrong!

In my due diligence efforts I did not discern that good old Sam, my new investor, was a recovering alcholic. Soon, Ward, the sleazy attorney, plied Sam with every kind of alcohol available. Ward, Hugh, and Sam came to my office. Ward began,

"Gardner, Sam has decided to vote his 20% interest with us, so we now control EME."

I looked at my associate, Sam. He, inebriated, really *sloshed*, stared at the floor. Marathon negotiations followed as I searched for a way to *forget the cheese and get out of the trap*. Ward interrupted my thinking,

"Our final offer to you is ten cents on a dollar for your $20,000 investment". (I had a policy that I would never invest more than $20,000, a lot of money at the time, in any one venture.)

"If you don't accept, we will issue enough shares of stock to dilute you down to nothing."

I agreed to accept "ten cents on a dollar". It was time to think *outside the box!* A light went on. I had found a solution! Electronic Manufacturing Engineers would save me!

The Company was in the process of leasing the only building available, owned by the government entity, PRIDCO (Puerto Rico Industrial Development Company). I visited my friend, the PRIDCO Director.

"Rolando, would you do me a favor? Could you require my written approval before you sign the new Lease with EME?"

I explained the situation and he agreed. The next day, Ward came to see me,.

"What is going on?"

"Well, Ward, your check is for only $2,000. There must be some misunderstanding, since "ten cents on a dollar means $1.10.""

"Gardner, you can't be that stupid. We'll just dilute you out!" I smiled,

"Do what you have to do, Ward!"

A few days later, a wide-eyed and docile Ward Dawbson brought me a check for $22,000 I glanced at it, and could not resist saying,

"Did we say *20 cents on a dollar* or *10 cents on a dollar?"*

His face fell. I accepted the $22,000 bank check. Several months later Ward succeeded in squandering all but $750,000 of my drunken friend Sam's fortune.

On one of the rare occasions in which he knew what was happening, Sam committed suicide because he felt he was penniless.

> **Rule**. *Never, ever, associate with a greedy person in business enter-prises. Do due diligence on every prospective Associate's past. Gauge the size of his or her* greed button. *The Spirit that guides entrepreneurs will tell you the level of greed in an individual. Greedy investors will nearly always win because they stay up at night to find ways to take over your assets, while you are sleeping .*

I trust you enjoyed and benefitted by this visit into my personal experiences of the *Fatal (or Near-Fatal) Distraction) of The Gold Ring, the False Doctrine of Infallibility, and the Greedy Associate.* Now, please join me in the following pages where you can learn *How to Become a Successful Entre-preneur and Make Bad Guys Finish Last.*

CHAPTER TWO |̲|

THE LAW OF THE HALF-BOOT

The Present Employment Debacle. The Law of the Half-Boot. Illustration Capsule One; Sowell Steel Company. Illustration Capsule Two; Equitech.

The Present Employment Debacle.

It has been said that, *An employee's value is the same to one company as it is to another.* In other words, ability, know-how, and experience qualify him or her for a lateral move to another firm at a similar level of responsibility, with the same or somewhat better compensation.

The obvious reality is that, during periods such as now, when companies are not hiring, this maxim is of little comfort to those terminated because of mergers, downsizing, etc. Many become involuntary entrepreneurs. They are forced into starting their own ventures or to purchase struggling companies. Others take temporary refuge in unemployment compensation, and may ultimately become resigned to lower-paying jobs. A few with sufficient resources may 'purchase a position' as a condition for making a relatively modest investment (usually $20,000 to $30,000) in small closely-held companies in urgent need of capital and management. Still others become consultants to small and medium-sized companies.

HOW TO MAKE BAD GUYS FINISH LAST

The Law of the Half-Boot

We have seen that termination of employment in large private and public corporations creates many *involuntary entrepreneurs*. Employees are often fired for breaking what I call the *Law of the Half-Boot*, which is usually not a written 'law' but is nonetheless real and inexorably enforced. It takes many forms and is most prevalent in privately-held corporations. Violations of the sometimes eccentric, nearly phobic, seemingly inconsequential policies of any given company sooner or later create *Involuntary External Entrepreneurs*. Dismissal will inevitably occur -- usually sooner rather than later.

The following Case Studies, each of which is as true as memory permits, will illustrate (better than a written explanation) how this *Law of the Half Boot* works:

Illustration Capsule One

Name: Sowell Steel Company • San Francisco, California.

Description: Manufacturer • Private Corporation.

Control: Major Shareholder, Edward L. Sowell

Urgent Need: New Vice President for Marketing

Policies: It was an unwritten law of Mr. Sowell that every executive will dress in a conservative dark suit, white shirt, and polished black Oxfords.

Scenario: A top-notch executive was recruited. He proved to be the right choice, and the sales of steel windows and *Steelite* buildings increased substantially under the new Vice

President.

Mr. Sowell noticed that this Vice President wore highly polished zippered *Bally* half-boots.

"Hal", the *old man* said, "I want to remind you of our dress code. If I make an exception to policy--that we all come to work in black dress Oxfords-- who knows what the Executives and Staff mght wear."

"Mr, Sowell, my black Half-Boots look like Oxfords. Nobody can tell the difference. For medical reasons, I need to wear them to support my ankles."

The truth was that he loved his Half-Boots, believing they brought him good luck. The President nodded thoughtfully, looking down at the floor. His lower lip thrust out (always a danger signal) and a wisp of hair, usually combed across his nearly bald pate, fell across one half-closed eye.

Nothing more was said. Hal became convinced that the *old man* would overlook his lack of compliance in footwear.

A year later Sowell called him into his office.

He asked Hal why he was not more of a *team player.* The old man had all his top executives interviewed by a *Friendly Psychologist* once a year. Mr Sowell then used the psychologist's report when he wanted to fire someone.

Hal was informed that his services were no longer required by Sowell Steel Company. The real reason, incredible as it might seem, was that he insisted on wearing his zippered Half-Boots. The VP still refused to mend his ways and join the ranks in their standard shiny black Oxfords. Hal stopped by my office and, with a rueful smile, said,

"I guess I violated the *Law of the Half Boot!*".

I felt sorry for the Vice President but completely ignored the danger, signalled by his abrupt departure. The Export Department, which I had created, expanded the company's market and profits for their line of utility buildings and steel sash.

At the end of the first year, Export Department earnings were substantial. Mr. Sowell surprised me with a generous bonus, which I used to purchase a new Buick convertible. When I saw him give a sour look toward my new car in the Company parking lot, the thought occurred to me that I was violating one of Sowell's unwritten policy,

> **Rule**. *No one, not even the Vice President will drive an automobile newer than the President's four year old black sedan.*

I had violated the inexorable Law of the Half-Boot.
But, I rationalized,
"The 'Old Man' likes and needs me!"

I was shaken when the CFO/Vice President, a tall, bitter, skinny fellow with a reddish face, came to my office. He really disliked me.

"Now, you've done it. Your days are numbered!"

Another year elapsed. The Export Department was the most profitable Division of the Company. It seemed a good time to ask for a substantial increase in salary and a percentage of the annual net profit, both of which were granted. I became the second-highest paid executive in the company. Though Mr. Sowell grumbled, he agreed. To my delight, I was to be paid, at year-end, a robust 7% of the annual net profits of the Export Department.

I was newly married and our dream home was being designed. All was well, except I had committed the *third and final violation of the Law of the Half-Boot.* which was:

Rule, *The President gives generous bonuses for extra performance. Nobody gets either ownership in the company or a percentage of profits.*

November arrived and I could hardly wait for my five figure check. I was called to the old man's office and met the Vice-President in the hall.

"You are history!" he said with evident relish.

Mr. Sowell studied the floor. His bald head lowered, retracted turtle-like between his shoulders. All five hairs had been combed carefully across his pate as if to deny their endangered state. Lower lip thrust out, he twiddled a yellow pencil between thumb and forefinger. Danger signals flashed.

"How much will we owe you next month?"

I named the fairly substantial amount and added,

"We had a very successful year in the Export Department, as you know."

"But," I added, "I certainly do not feel strongly about the amount. Would you prefer to adjust the amount?"

Not so much as moving his head or looking up, he replied,

"Nope! Not one red cent! For what I would have to pay you next month, I can get an Export Manager for two years!"

He looked up and, stabbing the pencil into the air,

"Instead of climbing the ladder one rung at a time -- and if a rung breaks you keep climbing upward -- you shot up like a rocket!"

The pencil emphasized the trajectory.

"You're *fired*!"

He reached for the intercom,

"Have Joe Bona come to my office,"

While we waited for Bona to arrive, Mr, Sowell read from the psychogist's report,

"Russell has a *dominant Mother. He is not a team player*" I was shocked and speechless.

"Yes, Mr, Sowell?"

Joe Boma came into the office.

—

Bona had been the President of his Class at Michigan State. When I interviewed him to be my Assistant, I asked him why he wanted the job.

"Because I want your job!"

I laughed,

"Then we'll make a great team, because you will push me!" We became good friends, shared an apartment.

—

"Joe, Gardner is leaving us and you will be the next Export Manager, with a substantial raise."

Bona looked at me,

"Is that right, Gardner?"

"Yes, but it's not Mr. Sowell's fault. I pushed too hard!"(Translation: *I violated too many Laws of the Half-boot*).

My Assistant, who had always wanted my job, turned to Sowell,

"If Gardner is leaving, so am I!"

I tried to get him to reconsider and the 'Old Man' told him about the generous bonus hewould receive. Joe was not to be persuaded to stay,

We left the office and cleaned out our desks, without a word. Once outside, my good friend flashed a big smile and saud,.

"I couldn't resist needling the Old Man. I was going to resign anyhow because I have a great offer to manage a paint factory in Mexico!"

I walked slowly to the building a few blocks away where my new bride managed an IBM tabulating unit (precursor of the computer) for the U.S. Army Corps of Engineers.

"What are you doing here so early?" she asked.

"The Old Man just fired me."

I had violated the *Law of the Half-Boot* -- not once but three times--and the price was inevitably exacted.

Illustration Capsule Two

Name:	Equitech • Los Angeles
Description:	Real Estate Investment and Management. Closely-Held Private Company.
Urgent Need:	Recruit a Leasing Manager.
Policies:	Executives protected their turf.

Scenario: The Company had recently acquired the Los Angeles World Trade Center. The CEO was a former missionary and good friend of mine. I recommended my son, a dynamic young man with little formal business experience but a knack for quick learning. He also showed early-on signs of *street smarts*.

He was hired as Leasing Manager. Within a matter of months, he substantially increased leasing revenue in the Los Angeles World Trade Center and was asked to manage the corporate office building, as well as two shopping centers.

HOW TO MAKE BAD GUYS FINISH LAST

Eager to advance in the company, he suggested ways to improve efficiency and profitability -- all of which were ignored by his supervisor, who, soon thereafter, became ill and was out of the office for several weeks. During his absence, the Leasing Manager acted on several of his previously ignored recommendations, which resulted in immediate and long-term benefits to the company.

Returning to the office and learning what had been done without his approval, the supervisor informed top management that,

"Russell is not a *team player*."

These have always been fashionable words to accelerate the departure of an employee. Several weeks later, my son, his street smarts alerted, checked his supervisor's daily calendar. He read the imprint of pages that had been torn off the calendar:"Fire Russell."

Russell had committed two violations of the *Law of the Half-Boot*; the price -- as always -- had to be paid.

After further corporate immersion, he recently retired as an accomplished entrepreneur, selling the assets of a multimillion dollar film conversion and packaging export business.

> **Rule**. *Before accepting employment*
> *with a private or public entity, it is im-*
> *portant to verify with former, as well*
> *as present, employees as to what unwritten*
> *laws of the Half-Boot are part of the*
> *entity's policies.This knowledge can*
> *help avoid unintentional violations of*
> *the Law of the Half-Boot. Yes, every*
> *entity has certain unwritten policies.*

CHAPTER THREE

THE SABER-TOOTHED TIGER AND THE ENTREPRENEUR

Saber-Toothed Tiger. Origin of the Word "Entrepreneur."
Contemporary Defnition. The Entrepreneurial Spirit. Internal
and External Entrepreneurs. The Corporate Promise. Invol-
untary Entrepreneur. The Corporate Game. The Voluntary
Entrepreneur

Scientists estimate that 3 million years ago, precursors of modern man had brains weighing one pound. After 2 million years the brain weight *more than doubled*. During those millennia, gnawed fossilized remains of their bones indicate that prehistoric man was regarded as a delicacy by the fearsome saber-toothed tiger.

Our ancestors survived by hiding in caves or in the primeval forest, nearly defenseless. Then one of them, while laboriously cleaning an animal skin with a fairly sharp stone, discovered that a very sharp scraping tool could be chipped from flint. Such ancient flint knives have been found in many areas of the world.

An individual may have been carrying this handy tool when attacked by a saber-toothed tiger. In desperation, he may have used the sharp implement to attempt to defend himself. This caused the tiger pain, and made it rethink its intended prey.

Later, while nursing tooth and claw wounds, the caveman may have considered his miraculous escape from the tiger. Though prehistoric man knew nothing of the basic entrepreneurial premise of *added value to existing technology*, it must have occurred to him that he now had a better weapon.

Survival instinct may have led to the discovery of the spear. By trial and error, he learned how to affix the flint knife to the shaft with a tough vine. He chipped a piece of flint into an arrow point and the spear was born. An entrepreneur appeared. The *value-added to his product (the knife)* was both measurable and life-changing.

The playing field was levelled, and man became the hunter instead of the hunted. Archeological finds of gnawed tiger bones attest to his entrepreneurial experience. As further proof, we note that his descendants outlived the saber-toothed tiger. Though the above story is anecdotal, man's entrepreneurial activity was, from the beginning, essential to survival.

Nearly all religions and traditions bespeak of some sort of Creation. Those of Judeo-Christian faiths affirm that Adam and Eve were entrepreneurs, who received celestial mentoring. The Book of Genesis records that Adam received instruction from Jehovah on how to till the earth, build altars, etc..

Whatever our belief, it cannot be disputed that we are recipients, to a greater or lesser degree, of an *entrepreneurial imprint* and *entrepreneurial spirit*. I also firmly believe that we receive *entrepreneurial genes* from our own ancestors. Not too long ago our more recent ancestors, the pilgrims and pioneers, were imbued with that driving entrepreneurial spirit necessary for survival.

The concept that the entrepreneurial spirit is somehow

imprinted in us is strengthened today by studies which find that if members of one's family have been entrepreneurial, the same spirit will often surface in the life of an offspring. Thus a son or daughter, grandson, or granddaughter-- more often than not-- becomes an active entrepreneur.

In some families, the spirit may lie dormant for years, even for generations, only to burst into flower in a successful entrepreneur.

Origin of the Word "Entrepreneur".

The word *entrepreneur* is of French origin. (I do not know if George W. Bush really said that the French have no word for 'Entrepreneur.) As early as the 15th century, a French citizen named *Cantillon* may have been the first to invent the word. His written definition has been preserved as

"The agent who purchases the means of production for combination into marketable products."

Three hundred years after Cantillon, another of his countrymen recorded a further definition: *J. B. Say* described the entrepreneur of his day as

"The organizer of a business firm central to its distributive and production functions."

Contemporary Definitions

One of the deans of modern entrepreneurial knowledge and study is *Joseph R. Mancuso* of the Center for *Entrepreneurial Studies and Management, Inc.* He is known as the Entrepreneur's entrepreneur-- and penned 24 books. He provides us with this insightful description, which you will have to read several times to fully comprehend,

"Essentially, entrepreneurs are innovators, combining different technologies or business concepts to produce marketable products or services. They fill-in the people,

financing, production, and marketing gaps by acquiring and assembling the necessary resources into newly created firms. But, foremost they are able to recognize potentially profitable opportunities to conceptualize the venture strategy, and to become the key force in successfully moving their ideas from the laboratory to the marketplace. Those who 'go it alone' are usually the firstborn in families having a self-employed parent, whose successes result in the entrepreneur's high need for achievement. Often formal education is pursued to the extent that a master's degree is obtained."

In *SUCCESS Magazine* we read, "You can't build a single psychological profile of the entrepreneur. There are too many examples that break the rules." (April 1993).

The Entrepreneurial Spirit

Perhaps, but there *are* ways to evaluate the management personality and style to identify entrepreneurial attributes. There are seemingly as many definitions of *Entrepreneur* and *Entrepreneurship* as there are writers who treat the subject.

As the 21st Century arrives, new and expanded definitions of entrepreneurs and entrepreneurship will undoubtedly come forth. For example, not many years ago few had logged on to the Internet. Now, few are those who do not use the Internet, New fortunes are being made every hour of the day by entrepreneurs creative and bold enough to exploit this technology.

Internal and External Entrepreneurs

Internal Voluntary Entrepreneurs are employees of private and public corporations and other institutions who feel the need to develop entrepreneurial attributes for the benefit of their employer. Until recently this was either discouraged by Corporate America, ignored, or given lip service. In recent years, enlightened employers have discovered that encouraging and nurturing quiescent entrepreneurship in select employees will result in measurable value-added benefits, in addition to better morale and less turnover.

There are a few companies specializing in seminars and one-on-one training, and books on the subject authored by well-known business writers. There is a curriculum in a number of universities designed to develop necessary entrepreneurial attributes in corporate employees.

External Voluntary Entrepreneurs are individuals who plan early in their careers to create a new venture or acquire an existing one. They typically work for a period in corporate or institutional entities until they have gained enough experience and seed capital to organize the new enterprise. This experience is important. There are those who believe a good idea and financial resources are sufficient to begin the business without such experience. There is a high failure rate in such 'PFTA' (plucked-from-thin-air) start-ups. Those who do succeed often pay a heavy price for their trial-and-error, on-the-job training.

The Corporate Promise--Involuntary Entrepreneur

Involuntary Entrepreneurs are men and women forced into entrepreneurial activity due to termination by the employer, or the realization that they are either unable or unwilling to continue to work for others. They number in the thousands. Corporations, private and public, are the greatest source of involuntary entrepreneurs. As noted, the breakdown of the traditional corporate promise of job retention and pension has forced many to take the entrepreneurial plunge.

HOW TO MAKE BAD GUYS FINISH LAST

Many factors, not the least of which is the increasingly complex global economy and proliferation of multinational companies, have adversely affected the corporate promise. Once sacrosanct company pension plans are now on the endangered species list and post-retirement health care commitments are diminished or disavowed. There are more broken or missing rungs on the corporate ladder than ever before.

Downsizing, re-engineering and rightsizing -- all euphemisms for termination -- continue unabated. Layoff bloodletting is a fact of life. Few companies are untouched. Fear of losing one's job in many areas is endemic.

That the unspoken corporate promise is no longer a reality is starkly apparent as employees in many areas, once terminated, are unable to find acceptable employment. Many find themselves thrust involuntarily into the marketplace, resulting in shotgun entrepreneurial marriages. Near-caesarean births of thousands of these new businesses have created tens of thousands of new jobs and a sharp upsurge in the strength of the marketplace.

The Corporate Game

Most company policy-makers believe that key executives, once they acquire sufficient capital, will leave to organize their own ventures. Enter the *Corporate Game*. The executive is informed that with each promotion, he or she will be *expected* to live on a scale befitting the position, to purchase a larger home in an upscale neighborhood, to entertain, to join an exclusive country club, to take expensive vacations, to place children in private schools, etc..

Expenses rise inexorably to match or surpass income. Asset formation, equity growth, and cash position are minimal. And today's executive is especially vulnerable to attrition in middle and top management positions resulting from mergers, acquisitions, or spin-offs. While the more fortunate are able to fund new ventures by golden handshakes and favorable asset bases, the majority are not so lucky. Not only do they have few assets, they are burdened with heavy debt, locked in to high standards of living by their former positions.

The Voluntary Entrepreneur

More and more corporate employees view their present employment as a stepping stone to entrepreneurship, following a preconceived plan. As soon as they acquire the ingredients of experience, seed capital, etc., they resign to organize the new venture. Should corporate downsizing, acquisitions, or mergers terminate their employment before the planned departure date, they launch their preemie first venture with minimal anxiety, since their plan is largely in place.

There are two main types of *voluntary entrepreneurs*: First are the corporate employees described previously who consciously prepare for their departure. These individuals will remain employed only until they acquire the necessary experience, know-how and capital to depart. Second are the individuals not well suited to the corporate environment for personality, political or other reasons.

Whether entrepreneurs be voluntary or involuntary, they share the same strong commitment to their new enterprises and, in an overwhelming number of cases, their spouses are supportive (although they may prefer a steady paycheck).

CHAPTER FOUR

MY EXPERIENCES IN STARTING THAT NEW VENTURE

Illustration Capsule One; Time Manufacturing. Illustration Capsule Two; Humphrey Associates. Inc. Illustration Capsule Three; INSA, Inc,. Illustration Capsule Four; The Cuban Supermarket Project. Illustration Capsule Five; Juan's Company

I llustration Capsule One:
Time Manufacturing Company.

My dream to be in Latin America again, and become involved in manufacturing, was about to be realized. I was in a meeting with the five Garcia brothers, owners of a very large construction materials business in Santurce, Puerto Rico. At the time they spoke no English.

"Do you need an interpreter, Mr. Russell?"

My street smarts signalled me.

"Yes, please,"

I replied, although I was fully bilingual in Spanish. The oldest brother, *Evaristo*, arrogant, swarthy. beetle-browed and heavy-set, held a smoking *cu-*

bano at eye level as he spoke,

"*A que nos ha mandado este pendejo, Moseley. No está ni seco detrás las orejas!*" (Why has Moseley sent us this jerk? He is not even dry behind the ears!)

I asked the interpreter to tell me in English what Don Evaristo had said.

"He says that he and the García brothers welcome you to Puerto Rico."

"Thank you."

And so it went, with further disparaging remarks from *Don Varo,* which my interpreter proclaimed were messages of warmth and welcome!

As the meeting came to a close, I asked permission to tell a story. I spun a long tale in Spanish. Several of the brothers were amused at Evaristo's discomfiture. Cigar held aloft, unmoving, mouth agape, he looked like a statue dedicated to Cuban cigars.

> **Rule**. *Always look for ways to find out what your associates or adversaries are really thinking. Knowing a language allowed me to do so. When I leave a business meeting, I close the door, then immediately reopen it and return to the room as if I had forgotten something. It is not uncommon to hear an uncomplimentary remark.*

I loved to tweak *Don Varo*, and once told him that I had heard that his attorney had found him sitting in front of the elevator at the Empire State Building, tears in his eyes, The attorney asked,

"*Que pasa, don Varo?*"

"Well, I keep trying to go to the 23rd floor and the elevator operator always lets me off at the 11th floor."

"Varo, let's get on the elevator again and you do what you have been doing."

They did and Evaristo said in a commanding voice,

"*Eleven!*"

which in Spanish means "Take us up!"

My nemesis moved his ever-present cigar to one side, gave me a sour look.

"*Rósel, tu y tus cuentos!*"

(Russell, you and your stories!)

My small family had been residing for two years in Garden Hills, on the outskirts of San Juan, Puerto Rico. I was employed as General Manager of Time Manufacturing Company, which produced and installed wood and aluminum jalousies (open louver windows) and doors.

My Puerto Rican stakeholders, the Garcías, became my good friends. But the U.S. partner become increasingly unfriendly toward me, finally hostile, and it took me awhile to find out why. He was a close friend of my Sales Manager, *Federico Villamilo*, who wanted my job. Villamilo, in a meeting on our front porch, once drew a very large handgun and pointed it me, saying,

"Si tu no me ayudas a conseguir acciones, yo te mato."(If you don't help me get stock in the Company, I'll kill you!) I replied,

"Federico, if I am still alive after your first shot, I will surely take you with me!"

An Associate intervened, and nothing further transpired. I suddenly realized *how seriously some individuals take business matters.* Later in my career I was to observe two suicides and a murder among my associates. (Jerry Mills, in his remarkable book, *The Danger Zone*, also tells of a suicide and murder among his clientelle.)

> **Rule.** *Never ignore or underestimate threats of bodily harm or worse, from business associates or others. Business-related murders and suicides are uncommon of course. But, just in case, be aware and vigilant at all times.*

Illustration Capsule Two:
Humphrey Associates, Inc.

With $7500 capital (then the cost of a starter home) proceeds from a non-compete agreement with the Garcías, it was time to become an *Involuntary Entrepreneur.*

Negotiating a buyout from the four owners of a moribund custom furniture factory in Trujillo Alto, Puerto Rico, I was to invest $5,000. The balance would be "x" if paid in one year, "y" in two years, or "z" in three years.

Two of the Sellers were my close friends. The third was a tough-minded Jewish attorney, Murray Oribstein. I had just taken over the factory, in a ramshackle building (without even an outhouse) when I received a letter from Murray, owner of the property. It read:

"Gardner, unpaid back rent of $2000 is owing on my building. I need your check or will have to evict you."

Nobody had brought up the matter of unpaid rent in our negotiations. Again, it was necessary to think outside the box and call on *street smarts.* I rented a factory and showroom space in upscale *Villa Caparra,* wired it with electrical "quick-connect" drop connections. On Thanksgiving morning Murray failed to appear on his balcony overlooking the factory, as he enjoyed his Holiday, and his ever vigilant watchman was on vacation.

A truck driver backed a container up to the building. In less than two hours, machinery, equipment and inventory were loaded into the container. As the truck pulled out, my crew and I stripped the building of all its electrical wiring.

We were operating in the new location the following Monday morning. The phone rang.

"Gardner, I have the same remedies at your new location!"

The Spanish have a saying. which I love,

"Para determinar el sexo del gato, hay que jalarlo por el rabo, pero cuidado que no te arañe." (To determine the sex of a cat one has to lift it up by the tail, but careful it doesn't scratch you).

"Murray, (the cat) come and get the keys. I don't have the $2,000. But I'll send you small monthly post-dated checks."

Several months later Murray called me.

"Gardner, you are the best businessman. I want you to join me in a project-- equal partners."

"Thanks for the offer, but 'yes, I guess not!'"

> **Rule**. *When forced to deal wiith crooked, greedy people, call on your best street smarts and creative outside-the-box thinking. The result might not be pretty but you can save the day.*

I ceased manufacturing custom furntiture and obtained approval by the FHA (Federal Housing Administration) to extend their program to finance kitchens as part of new homes in Puerto Rico. The business grew and I became involved with four wonderful associates in construction.

We first built 120 homes, then 1000 precast tiltup houses, a shopping center, a 10 story high-rise. etc..

It was time to execute my Exit Plan. I sold my equities to the other stakeholders for $125,000 (a princely sum at the time).

Illustration Capsule Three
INSA, INC.

There were no Growth Equity or Venture Capital firms in Puerto Rico. Together with an Associate we organized a mini-venture capital fund, and INSA, INC was born. INSA soon acquired control of *Rico Plastics, Manhattan (Fiber) Broom Company, and Electronic Manufacturing Engineers.*

My associate convinced me, against my better judgement, that we needed additional investors in INSA, Inc. Enter Sam, a lovely, slim, bespectacled, sun-bronzed, balding young man who had sailed his yacht from the East to Puerto Rico. The complete story of Sam is told elsewhere in this book, leading to his suicide when in a lucid moment he learmed that his multi-million dollar fortune had shrunk to $750,000.

Illustration Capsule Four:
The Cuban Supermarket Project.

I liquidated my holdings in INSA, INC. and with several new associates became involved in a large building company. At one time I owned 25% of a shopping center, a high-rise apartment complex, and 1000 homes,

My associates asked me to travel to Havana, Cuba, and research the possibility of building and operating a modern suppermarket there.

I shall never forget the somber, almost palpable feeling of despair in the air as I revisited that lovely island. It came to me forcefully.

"Fidel Castro is going to come down out of the mountains and he will win!"

I was depressed. I wandered into the Casino at the *Hotel Nacional*. I never gambled, and was shocked to suddenly find myself sitting at a roulette table, $300 in the hole. Really upset at my foolishness, I moved to a Blackjack table, and slowly, carefully, thankfully 'broke even'.

Back In San Juan, I presented a negative report to my associates concerning the Cuban venture. One of the stakeholders, who wanted to be the Manager, convinced several others to build the Supermarket anyhow. It was one of the first businesses expropriated by Castro when he took over.

The Supermarket Manager, my friend and Associate, committed suicide. Unbelievable. Suicide is a permanent solution to a temporary problem.

llustration Capsule Five:
Juan's Company

My friend Juan, a Guatemalan with a fine young family, had a thriving business in Guatemala City. When I asked about him, I was informed that he had discovered that his two Associates were embezzling thousands of dollars from the Company. He said he was going to confront them.

His friends asked him not to meet alone that night with the two embezzlers. He said,

"I can handle them!"

The following morning, he was found on the floor of the elevator, dead. He had been strangled with his own necktie.

> **Rule**: *Never underestimate the seriousness with which some individuals view business interests. Perceived adverse events can and do lead to suicide and murder or serious bodily harm. Al - ways be aware and vigilant.*

CHAPTER FIVE

THE ENTREPRENEURIAL MIND AT WORK

Illustration Capsule One; The Better Mousetrap. That 'Great Idea' is Like the Baby Leatherback Turtle. One in a Thousand Makes it. Personal Evaluation Checklists. The "Creative Innovations" Attribute. Illustration Capsule Two; A Better Beverage Cart . Illustration Capsule Three; The Mother-in-Law Pod

I llustration Capsule One ; A Better Mousetrap
A word about inventors, inventor-entrepreneurs and would-be inventors. As for the latter, it is rare to find a man or woman, old or young, who does not have a 'great idea' for some kind of an invention. The unfortunate reality is that at least 90% of these concepts do not bear up under scrutiny, usually because the product is not viable and/or there is little or no market of substance.

The old maxim was:

Build a better mousetrap and the world will beat
a path to your door."

The new premise is:

"Nearly anything that can be sold, can be made."

New products become irrelevant in the absence of a *pre-tested market niche.* For instance, there will probably never be a truly *better mousetrap* because it could not compete with the traditional wood-mounted trigger-bail device.

A possible exception might be the invention of a multiple entry trap that would instantaneously vaporize the rodent in some fashion. The fastidious or squeamish would buy such a trap because cost would be no object. But, this would probably account for only a thin slice of the available market.

My farmer-uncle in Jensen, Utah, once showed me how to make a do-it-yourself mousetrap. He inserted a stiff wire through the eyelets holding the bail of a milk pail, partly-filled it with water. He then squeezed a lump of damp bread dough around the wire at its midpoint.

Mice easily maintained their balance along the wire, crawled onto the dough which proved to provide no clawhold. The wire promptly rotated and dropped the mouse into the water below. New innovations have not created a better mousetrap.

But, a different technology has taken over. A few traps cling forlornly to a corner of the store shelf, which is now filled with a variety of poison baits. No matter that the rodent will die in the wall and make its 'presence known' for days or weeks.

> **Rule**. *The entrepreneur nust be certain there is a viable market niche for the value-added product or service. Avoid.becomng obsessed with your product or idea. (A client spent a fortune on a scissors lift, which had already been invented).*

That 'Great Idea' is Like the Baby Leatherback Turtle. One in a Thousand Makes it.

One of our national characteristics is that nearly every adult has (1) at least one idea for a business (usually not viable), and (2) an opinion, well-informed or not (usually not), about almost any subject.

It had not become apparent that I would soon become an *External Involuntary Entrepreneur.* I wondered why I did not seem to be suited to the corporate environment. My peer group unsheathed their flashing back-stabber knives from the moment I first said hello to them. Apparently, I represented a threat to them. Without realizing it, I was learning a great deal about business and would soon be ready to become an *involuntary entrepreneur.*

I had already made the decision to change my career path from export or domestic sales to manufacturing. So, when Tim Moseley of Dalmo Victor, San Carlos, California asked me to counsel him on a start-up manufacturing company in Puerto Rico, I eagerly accepted. I visited the island and received an offer from Moseley and the Puerto Rican shareholders to become General Manager of *Time Manufacturing Company.* I called Dorothy on Sunday.

"If I am to salvage Time Manufacuring (see Chapter One), I must stay.There is a boat leaving Friday for Puerto Rico."

She sold the house on Monday, had the furniture and car picked up for the docks on Wednesday, stayed with friends that night. Then she showed our eldest daughter to her grandparents, arriving in San Juan two weeks later.

There followed more than 20 years of successful, challenging and often exhilarating experiences as an Entrepreneur: manufacturer, consultant and inventor-entrepreneur under the Federal income tax-free *Operation Bootstrap* of the Government of Puerto Rico.

Personal Evaluation Checklists

There are detailed personality profiles and evaluations for would-be entrepreneurs, compiled by leading authorities in psychology, human resources and relations. Their findings are supported by exhaustive studies that can be meaningful and valuable. They use formulas and variables in varying degrees of difficulty which may be hard, if not almost impossible, for the layman (or myself) to comprehend and implement. But the reader might find some of them valuable. There are also detailed lists of attributes, characteristics and habits of entrepreneurship which might (or not) be helpful in a self-evaluation.

Studies have shown conclusively that the *majority of individuals can learn to be entrepreneurs*. In addition to courses in many two and four year colleges, there are a number of *Centers for Entrepreneurial Studies and Management*, such as the one directed by Joseph R. Mancuso.

The "Creative Innovations" Attribute

Lifelong amassing of knowledge from experience, observation and a variety of seemingly unrelated sources can create an amazing mental storehouse, from which technologies can be combined for creative enhancements to existing products, or innovative new products or services. The mind of the venturer constantly probes for possible products and market niches in light of all the accumulated knowledge. A few examples follow,

Illustration Capsule Two ; A Better Beverage Cart
On long flights, (they don't feed you if the flight is less than four hours long), I observed flight attendants as they struggled with the heavy, unwieldy metal food and beverage carts.

I know of airlines which have been sued for resultant back injuries. There is obviously a *need* for an improved cart. The project wa soon outlined on the back of an envelope.

Project: To replace heavy, unwieldy metal food and beverage carts with lighter ones of molded fire-resistant plastic, with indents to spare passenger elbows. Carts should be electric, with push-bar control of brakes, and controlled by a wire or tape concealed under the aisle carpet (using fork-lift technology).

I penciled a note:

Research requirements for sealed motors, as well as FAA and other necessary approvals. Then I set the *Good Idea* aside, because the approval process could take years.

Illustration Capsule Three; The Mother-in-Law Pod

I browsed through a magazine, found an article about housing difficulties for the elderly, and the economic and physical need for families to continue living in the same house.

The creative process began anew and I scribblrd notes.

Project: Develop a free-standing, factory-built Mother-rin-Law Apartment. Possibly of geodesic design. Name it *'Mother-in Law Pod'?* Must have all amenities including kitchen, living-dining area, bedroom and bath. Special electric-powered wheel chair which, at the touch of a button (using warehouse forklift technology), will follow a magnetic tape under the carpet either to the kitchen, the bedroom or the bathroom. Use wheelchair unit (already in production) which will tilt vertically and allows a person to 'stand' upright, even though legs will not support the body.

Then the mother-in-law can wheel her power chair into the kitchen, touch a button and be raised erect. This will provide a powerful psychological boost because, once vertical, she can prepare meals and feel almost normal.

The brainstorming continued.

Parents and in-laws inevitably become enfeebled, yet should be able to take a normal bath, luxuriating in a tub, and not a sitting bath. Design, from existing fork-lift or physical therapy technology, a device which will position a person horizontally over the tub and gently lower him or her to a reclining position and reverse at the touch of a buttons.

I scribbled some numbers.

"A comfortable pod could be built and sold for $50,000 to $100,000. See if Pod will qualify for FHA or equity mortgage financing.

(Note: Once a door is cut into a wall of the children's home, and the pod fastened to the structure, it should qualify for FHA and other long-term financing. When the parents die, the pod can easily be removed.)

The typical entrepreneur considers one or more possible value-added projects almost daily. Most are discarded for reasons of marketing, timing or onerous and expensive government regulation requirements (as in the case of the contemplated new food and beverage airline cart).

There is no scientific theory of creative innovation, but we know that inquiring minds constantly seek innovative opportunities. It is an important skill to develop, and a rare gift to learn, systematic innovation. The key is to recognize and identify an apparent market need, verify what improvements might be introduced for a better product or service. The best new products or services may well emerge from the unexpected, even the apparently incongruous, to better meet a perceived product or service need.

CHAPTER SIX

ENTREPRENEURS AND ENTREPRENEURSHIP
Internal Entrepreneurs. The Corporate Promise and the Involuntary Entrepreneur. Behind the Successful Entrepreneur. The Sole Proprietor. Entrepreneurs In Transition. The Dog-in-the-Manger, Would-Be Entrepreneur and Other "Wannabes"

Internal Entrepreneurs
In recent years, enlightened employers have discovered that by encouraging and nurturing *quiescent entrepreneurship* in select employees, the company will enjoy additional value-added products and services, and increased profits. A side benefit is better morale and less turnover among valuable employees.

More and more companies specialize in entrepreneurial seminars and one-on-one training. There is a plethora of books on entrepreneurs and entrepreneurship. Many of them are authored by well-known business writers. Perhaps the most prolific is Joseph Mancuso, with more than 24 books published.

There are *Centers for Entrepreneurial Studies* in most major universities. Not a few have courses for corporate employees to develop entrepreneurial skills and attributes.

External Voluntary Entrepreneurs are individuals who plan early in their careers to create a new venture or acquire an existing one. They typically work for a period in corporate or institutional entities until they have gained enough experience and seed capital to organize the new enterprise.

This interim experience is vital. There are those who believe that a good idea and financial resources are sufficient tools for the budding entrepreneur to begin the new venture. There is a high failure rate in such 'PFTA' (plucked-from-thin-air) start-ups.

New enterprises sans prior business experience often pay a heavy price for their trial-and-error, on-the-job learning.

The Corporate Promise and the Involuntary Entrepreneur

Involuntary Entrepreneurs are men and women forced into entrepreneurial activity due to termination by the employer, or the realization that they are either unable or unwilling to continue to work for others. They number in the thousands.

Corporations, private and public, are the greatest source of *involuntary entrepreneurs*. As noted, the breakdown of the traditional corporate promise of job retention and pension has forced many to take the entrepreneurial plunge.

Many factors, not the least of which is the increasingly complex global economy and proliferation of multinational companies, have adversely affected the corporate promise. Once sacrosanct company pension plans are now on the endangered species list, and post-retirement health care commitments are diminished or disavowed. There are more broken or missing rungs on the corporate ladder than ever before.

Downsizing, re-engineering and rightsizing — all euphemisms for the issuance of pink slips — continue unabated. Layoff bloodletting is a fact of life.

Few companies are untouched. Fear of losing one's job in many areas is endemic.

That the unspoken corporate promise is no longer a reality is starkly apparent. For decades, employees who left their Company were able to move laterally (basically at the same or somewhat higher salary level) to another Company. The hiring drought has largely eliminated this option. It is a sobering fact that,in many areas, second and even third level employees, once terminated, are unable to find acceptable employment.

Many terminated employees now find themselves thrust involuntarily into the marketplace, resulting in shotgun entrepreneurial marriages to new independent enterprises. The good news is that there are near-caesarean births of thousands of these new businesses, which have created tens of thousands of new jobs and an upsurge in the strength of the marketplace

Behind the Successful Entrepreneur

It has been said that a successful entrepreneur is the product of one or more failures. And it is also said, albeit facetiously, that behind the successful entrepreneur (most are married) is a mother-in-law who cannot believe he can succeed, and possibly never will. There is also a spouse who, even though she supports his or her mate in their new venture, will for many years miss the regular paycheck.

Vital Entrepreneurial Attributes Can Be Learned.

In this book are keys to prepare for, then embark on that *new venture,* and hopefully, enjoy the success and rewards, both financial and personal, that entrepreneurship offers.

However, if the first venture is a failure or runs into serious trouble, there are proven ways to keep assets intact and *Make Bad Guys Finish Last* so one can begin again.

Although experts differ on what constitutes an entrepreneur, they do agree that the *basic attributes critical to entrepreneurship can be learned.* It is now recognized that even a person working in a so-called 'trustee' or 'refining' capacity typical of management in large private or public companies might blossom (if given the opportunity) into successful activity as an *internal entrepreneur.* Such individual contributions can be of significant value once these skills are recognized and encouraged by the organization.

Our emphasis will be upon the *external entrepreneur* — the person who independently develops products or services which answer a specific and unattended need in the marketplace, usually in a definite and measurable niche.

We will not dwell on either the meteoric rise of those few who have ascended to Fortune 500 or 1000 status, large private and public corporations controlled by entrepreneurs, or multi-millionaires whose success is so well-chronicled by the media. Nor will we treat further the aspects of internal entrepreneurs performing within large companies.

The Sole Proprietor

Though the sole proprietor is vital to our communities and their economic fabric, he or she may not necessarily be entrepreneurial. The requirements, traits and attributes of the owner of an existing business are less demanding than those required for most entrepreneurial start-ups. Basic management skills are usually sufficient. A majority of these "Mom and Pop" stores, have known and measured parameters. They focus on the available customer base and are usually retail in nature. Little new value is added.

An entrepreneur might view retail product or service outlets as stifling and restrictive. He or she envisions that waiting at a location all day for customers to arrive, busying oneself with records, inventory, point-of-sale displays, shrinkage and obsolescence, is abhorrent to the entrepreneurial nature.

In my mind, waiting for a customer to wander in is somehow akin to the spider that spins its web in a likely place and waits for its victims. In the retail store, the owner tends the web, rearranges and renews filaments and waits.

This scenario of waiting is the antithesis of the creative entrepreneur who is driven to innovate, reach out and create new value. Many sole proprietors, however, transition to entrepreneurship.

Entrepreneurs In Transition

There are sole proprietors who become outstanding entrepeneurs by exploiting new niches. For example, when the sole owner of a store or service business identifies a niche for expansion of products or services, or develops the business into a franchise operation or a chain of stores, a new entrepreneur is born and new value created.

Examples abound of former sole proprietors who are *entrepreneurs in transition*. Like the ice cream maker who began with one Washington D.C. Hot Shoppe, and now owns and franchises hundreds of hotels.

Or the housewife who first opened one cookie store and now has hundreds of franchised and company-owned stores.

And Sylvan Goldman, the man who borrowed from his in-laws to buy the first grocery store, invented the nesting grocery cart and created an empire of supermarkets, shopping centers and more. The author was one of his associates in substantial ventures in Puerto Rico.

> **Rule***: Entrepreneurs can rarely be happy in sole proprietorships, but sole proprietors can and do become successful, happy, entrepreneurs.*

The Dog-in-the Manger Would-Be Entrepreneur And Other "Wannabes".

Most of us know of one or more would-be inventors who, convinced of the value of their creation, doggedly continue to refine and perfect their inventions over months and years. They live off savings, loans from family, banks and others, and are doomed to failure in the absence of a viable market for their product or service.

There is also a small group of inventors who rarely start a new business, because they can never quite bring forth a production prototype. They constantly strive to improve the product. They continue to tinker, create and recreate, long after the item is ready for the market. Like the would-be inventor, they are possessive and reflect a dog-in-the-manger attitude.

They cannot or will not do what is required to transform the invention into a viable business. Yet, they will not let anyone else provide the services needed.

There are also the hundreds and even thousands of dedicated and sometimes inspired inventors who envision, create and bring a series of successful products or service to market.

Some are *pure inventor-entrepreneurs*, content to develop production prototypes, then license the technology to a manufacturer, and receive license fees and royalties. They then move on to new challenging inventing opportunities.

In a class by themselves are the *inventor-entrepreneurs* who also share a devotion to their invention, yet their true desire is to devote all necessary assets, time and efforts to bring it to market. They often manufacture prototypes in their garages or modest rental spaces.

When a production prototype is debugged and field tested, they set up a small shop to manufacture the final product, and market the product themselves. They fervently try to retain 100 percent of the equity interest.

The author was an inventor-entrepreneur, with several design patents, the inventor-entrepreneurs tend to expand rapidly and require additional working capital. They become prime targets of the *Bad Guys*.

CHAPTER SEVEN

HOW TO START THAT NEW VENTURE

Nuts and Bolts. Select a Name For the Business, Register the Name, Select the Legal Structure, Bookkeeping and Accounting. Step One - Select Tangibles or Intangibles. Step Two - Select a Value-Added Product. Step Three - Create a Business Plan. Step Four - Determine the Available Market. Field Test The Prototype. Step Five - Keeping the Day Job. Step Six - Lease the Factory Space. Perfect Your Deferred Compliance. Step Seven - The Manufacturing Subcontractor. Step Eight - Low Business Profile. Full Compliance. Step Nine - Determining the Manufacturing Cost. Step Ten - Creative Marketing is a Must.

Nuts and Bolts
The entrepreneur learns, sometimes to his or her chagrin, that in the start-up phase of the new venture, all the detail work is his or hers. There is no one to delegate to. This is a rude awakening for many a NEWCO owner. The work hours hover around 70 per week. Here are some of the nuts and bolts that must be in place before operations begin,

Select a Name for the Business

Try to select a name that describes the product, with a Resonating Acronym. This appears easy but is not. I never tried to create a company name after I selected the name *Intercore Industries, Inc.* as my umbrella company for various industries. The first phone jarred me to reality,

Hey, Gardner, how's *Intercourse Industries* doing?" accompanied by a guffaw.

The offending registration, letterhead, invoices, etc. went into the trash can. In its place, *Antilles Wood Industries (AWICO)* was born.

Register the Name. Select the Legal Structure

One way to determine if the NEWCO Name selection is available, is to click on your State's Department of State and review the list of similar company names. If the name you selected is already in use, back to the drawing board.

One of the requirements for Registration of the Company with the Department of State is that the Legal Structure of NEWCO be declared in the Registration Document. The selection of the most advantageous Legal Struucture for you is of primary importance.

> **Rule:** *Before you select the initial legal structure for NEWCO, review the advantages and disadvantages of each with an attorney and with a competent accountant. If you forecast in your Business Plan extended period of operating losses, (years, not months), then perhaps an S-Corporation (which allows corporate losses to be deducted on your Personal Income Tax Return) might be advisable, or a C- Corporation with a Subchapter S-Election accomplishes the same purpose. LLCs have become popular*

Bookkeeping and Accounting

If either you are your spouse are comfortable with

numbers, you can create your own set of books (records). General Ledger, Income and Expense, etc. Visit your software store for a Demo. Research the Internet for the Simplest Program. (Microsoft, Quicken,etc.) Select your Chart of Accounts and post every transaction as a line item in the designated account.

If you or your spouse do not feel comfortable doing the bookkeeping, write the applicable account number from the Chart of Accounts on each document (check stub, invoice, account payable, etc.). Place all the documents each month in a box and take them to a young struggling accountant, and he or she will produce your monthly Operating Statement. Or, pay a Bookkeeper to come in one day a week and input the data and take off the Profit and Loss Statement and Balance Sheet on or before the 10th of each month. The latter choice may be the best until the growth of your Enterprise justifies a paid bookkeeper/accountant.

Step One - Select Tangibles or Intangibles

The budding entrepreneur must first of all select his or her preferred market area, whether it be in the *Tangible or Intangible Markets*. Few, if any, entrepreneurs are effective in both markets. By definition, *Tangible Sales* include products one can touch and feel. They usually have a finite purpose and are manufactured, molded, cast, or assembled products.

Tangible Sales are divided into two main areas, *Smokestack and Consumer products*. Most, if not all, sales to industry (Smokestack) are wholesale, while markets for consumer products may be either *Wholesale or Retail*. Your expertise must determine the area of concentration. *Intangibles* include insurance, stock trading, Internet activites, etc..

The author found early-on that he could not easily sell

Intangibles, Therefore he devoted his entire business life to the manufacture and assembly of products, This book, therefore, concentrates on *Tangibles.* For those whose interest and expertise lies in *Intangibles,* the basic precepts of how to start a new venture are the same.``

Step Two - Select a Value-Added Product

The Tangible Product must either be new and command a ready market, or be a better product than those on the market, by virtue of *value-added technology.* The overall governing factor in selecting the product is, simply stated, whether anyone will buy it. So, it must be better than anything on the market and must be competitively priced.

Step Three - Create a Business Plan

A new venture without a Business Plan is like a ship without a rudder. There are Business Plan software programs galore in Computer Stores and on the Internet, ranging from relatively simple software programs for under $100 to complex and downright unfriendly ones. You can download the selected software program to your computer, but be aware that the tutorials are written by software engineers and are hard to understand.

I strongly recommend that you visit your local computer store, and enlist the help of the usually knowledgeable sales tech. Have him or her recomend the best Business Plan, then open it in the store's computer and have the tech walk you through it. Then, if you still have trouble making the program work in your computer, don't fight it. Call your guru and have him set up all the necessary parameters, the Chart of Accounts, and your first spreadsheet. Excel is the usual program for a working spreadsheet. Enter each month's name on the columns, from left to right. The first line will read "Total Projected Monthly Net Sales (Less Discounts)".

Under the first month list all the Fixed Costs, and a line for a total. Then list all the Selling Expenses for the month, and totals. Then list General and Administrative Expenes and a subtotal. Finally, list the Gross Profit % and amount.

The last line on the Spreadsheet will be Net Profit Before Taxes (NPBT). For a successful small business, this should equate to a minimum of 30% of Net Sales. Your working Spreadsheet will have 12 monthly columns, plus a 13th column for annual totals of line items. Have your software tech or guru teach you the magic of Ranges and the ways to create *What-Ifs*. For example: What if Annual Sales are 20% less than projected? What impact would that have on the bottom line, etc.

Step Four - Determine the Available Market. Field Test the Prototype

One of the most common errors made by the budding entrepreneur is to do less than *due diligence* to prove the *market niche* for his or her new product or service. How does one quantify the available market? The answer is: to exhaust all public and private sources of information and, at the same time, pursue non-traditional sources of information, such as the Internet, Trade Associations (there is a Trade Association for nearly every product), competition, etc.. Calls to Vendors who sell to your competitors are often fruitful.

One of my most successful entrepreneurial ventures might contribute to the Reader's mind-broadening, An inventor and I organized a filter-strainer manufacturing entity named *Vu-Flow Filters Company*, in Melbourne, Florida, it was a known fact that sand, shell, and grit were shortening the life of pumps on lawn sprinkling systems. Existing filters were inadequate. Together with my inventor-associate, we devised a filter-strainer with 50% to 60% additional filtering capacity, competitive in price with existing filters on the market. The prototype was field-tested successfully for six months.

> **Rule**: *Always field-test your prototype for six months to a year, prior to going to market. There is rarely a prototype that does not require tweaking or actual modifications after being field-tested. The production model must have zero surprises.*

The first filter was initially made from shelf PVC and Lexan parts. The housing was a threaded pipe cap on one end, and an elbow on the other. In between was a clear Lexan pipe, cut to size and glued to the housing. The filter element was comprised of a slotted PVC tube, wrapped with a sleeve of filtering material, affixed with hot glue to the element. The cost to produce each filterwas $9.43.From the first profits, we had injection molds made at a cost of $12,000. and reduced the cost to under $3.53 each.

Step Five - Keeping the Day-Job

I do not believe I need to enlarge on this, except to restate that you need, for NEWCO's sake, to cover your living expenses from outside sources; in other words keep your *day jobs*. Take nothing, not one penny, out of the Company for yourself. And, above all, do not visit the cash register for a few dollars. If need be, you may establish a small Petty Cash Fund for incidentals. A receipt must back ever petty cash disbursement. .

> **Rule**: *Always keep your day job while*

you start and initially grow the new busi-
ness. A common error is for the entrepre-
neur to resign his or her employment to
devote full-time to the new venture. The
standard of living cannot be lowered,
so there is an immediate start-up load
on NEWCO of four to eight thousand
dollars a month. It is, obiously, even
worse when two associates leave their
their employment and live off the
embryonic venture. The resultant finan-
cial burden has an immediate negative
cash flow effect. The Stakeholders are
forced to immediately look for OPM,
and to sacrifice equity to do so,

Back to the filter business. From the first profits, injection molds were made, The Lexan housing became one closed-end threaded piece and the molded PVC housing held a reveal to receive an "O"-Ring seal. Now the filter element could be cleaned from time to time, by unscrewing the Lexan filter cover. The production costs plummeted to less than $4 per filter.

Step Six - Lease the Factory Space. Perfect Your Deferred Compliance

Once the product has passed the field test, with the production prototype ready and the market niche identified, strive for anonymity. Rent a bare-bones space. A good place to start the new venture is in a Storage Warehouse which caters to small businesses.

Foremost in your mind must be *deferred compliance of social additions.* Your new business cannot initially stand the impact of demands of various governmental agencies inspectors and their *social additions*, such as Social Security (FICA), Workmens' Compensation, OSHA, etc. These additions can add from 30% to 50% of total salaries.

Check with Social Security and the Internal Revenue Service to determiine the maximum number of employees allowed without filing. At present, under certain conditions, up to three employees require no filings.

Step Seven - The Manufacturing Subcontractor

This step is vital for inital cash preservation. You subcontract the manufacturing to a competent person, utilizing piecework wherever possible. Never designate the Sub-Contractor as an Independent Contractor, because the Internal Revenue Service has a 12 point criteria which an IC must meet. (Example, to meet IRS requirements, the IC must have "several customers" to qualify.)

The Subcontractor Agreement will recite that the Sub will be responsible for *all social additions* of his employees. Whether he complies or not with existing regulations, you do not know. However, if he is caught in non-compliance, you will be liable under Agency Law.

Step Eight - Low Business Profile. Full Compliance

The initial *deferred compliance* and *owners not taking anything out of NEWCO* has an amazing cash-flow effect. In the *Vu-Flow Filters* example, NPBT on the first 2500 filters, sold to warehousing distrbutors, totaled approximately $12.000. This covered the cost of injection molds, which allowed us to earn *three times* more per filter.

Building cash flow from profits is a powerful financial tool. The *ongoing financial needs of the business are largely met from profits, after provision for income taxes.*

There are several business realities. Your wholesale customers never come to you, you always go to them. Therefore you do not need a showplace office. A *window-shaker*

A/C (in Florida), a desk, two chairs (bought at auction) and a file cabinet suffice.

Do not put a sign on your rented space. The Post Office will find you. The busily engaged emissaries (inspector/enforcers) of local, state, and federal government agencies will not find you, or will ignore you, as simply another one-man business -- ready to disappear if contacted.

As soon as there is sufficient growth in NEWCO, move into the phase of *full compliance with social additions* Employ a Working Foreman, hire employees (using piecwork wherever possible) and cancel the Subcontractor Agreement. Register NEWCO with FICA, Workmen's Comp, Osha, etc. and patiently endure and comply with their demands.

Step Nine -Determining the Manufacturing Cost

Determine the true cost to manufacture the product. An easy way to do this is to list in detail on an Excel Spreadsheet the costs to produce, say, 2000 units each month. Start with what we call *Direct Costs* such as Labor, Materials, Factory Supplies, and Purchase Parts

Then, list in equal detail all the *Indirect Costs*, which consist of General and Administrative Expenses (G&A): Rent, Telephone. Office, Sales and Management Salaries, Power, Water, Waste R emval, Ins urance, Shipping, e tc..

Step Ten - Creative Marketing is a Must.

Using traditional marketing methods is costly, ranging from $50,000 to $100,000. These are impossible numbers for the new entrepreneur to digest. The salvation lies in *personal creative marketing. Vu-Flow* covered the total Florida market for filter-strainers with one stocking distributor. How to expand into the National Market?

I reasoned that only areas with *dirty* water (contaminated

with silt, shell, grit, etc.) would utilize our filters. As part of my inital due diligence, I called the *United States Department of Agriculture*. Did they have information on dirty water locations in other areas? Yes! There was a complete study in their files, with maps of dirty water locations.

Obviously *Vu-Flow Filters* would have a substantial market nationwide. Then I pondered how to market the filter nationally. I was not prepared to invest the $50,000, quoted by marketing specialists, and my associate had no discretionary funds. It also goes without saying that such a cash commitment offended my policy of minimal capitalization of the company. It was again time to think *outside-the-box*.

I obtained a list from a Trade Association of the major Stocking Warehouses (companies that buy products and warehouse them for sale to the retail market) of nipples, pumps, etc. in each identified market area. Utilizing this list, I prepared *Wholesale Distributor Agreements* with atttractive pricing and discount sheets and flyers.

Using my computer's "mail-merge" function, I was able to personalize the "package" to the owner of each of the major stocking warehouse companies. The package included a detailed Marketing Agreement, signed by the filter company President. Part of it read:

"You have been selected as a Stocking Distributor for *Vu-Flow Filters Company*. In order for you to represent *Vu-Flow Filters Company* in your area, please sign and return one copy of this Agreement, and your initial stocking order for 500 filters."

Using the "mail-merge" function on my computer sent identical signed agreements to as many as four companies in the same city. The first to return the signed agreement, became a *Vu-Flow Filters Company* Sticking Distributor.

From that first mailing we received orders for 2500 filters! Our new California Distributor called, incensed.

"You sent the same contract to one of my competitors!"

"What are you complaining about? You were selected!" I would have liked to have seen his face had he known that I actually mailed 4 agreements to his city! Years later, the key stocking distributors that were selected from that one mailing still carry the *Vu-Flow Filters Co.* line, and represent 80% of annual filter sales,

Thus, at one 'fell stroke', as the saying goes, we proved out the market niche, and did a complete marketing job for less than $5,000. We were soon able to take out *deferred compensation* averaging $50,000 a year apiece. Then, I turned *Vu-Flow Filters Co.* management over to my son, who implemented our Exit Plan and sold *Vu-Flow Filters Co.* for $750,000, vs. total paid-in capital of $6,000, a truly astronomical ROI (Return on Investment).

> **Rule**: *Some 'butcher-boy' tools. Accounts Receivable will amount to at least 15% of net sales. At $500,000 annual sales, for example, there must be enough working capital to 'carry' $75,000 in accounts receivable alone.*

Remember, you must determine if there is a market for the value-added product or service and a *guesstimate of* possible sales per annum in your market area.

> **Rule** *Always do your due diligence to gauge the size of the Market Niche for your value-added or new product or service. Research traditional government*

*and private studies and reports. Evaluate
the strength of your competition. If your
product utilizes shelf parts, contact
the parts mnufacturer for market information. More often than not, these
companies are knowlegeable in your
market and may even sell parts to
your compeittors. Immerse yourself
in the Internet and Research Trade Associations. Do not begin the venture until
you have a reasonable knowledge of
the available market.*

Then, find ways to avoid costly standard marketing approaches. Be constantly on the lookout for new applications for your products. For instance, Vu-Flow Filters
Company happened to fill a need for the then budding
drip irrigation industry. By inventing a filtering element
down to 5 microns, tiny emitter holes remained open in
drip irrigation lines, .

Constantly search out new products and application for
existing product. Never get caught in the trap of staying
with a cherished product or service during a diminishing
market. Unless you have deep pockets, do not select a
capital-intensive product with expensive machinery and
equipment requirements.

Notable Quotes from Peter F. Drucker
*The practice of Innovation: Innovation is the
specific tool of entrepreneurs, the means by
which they exploit change as an opportunity
for a different business or a different service.*

HOW TO MAKE BAD GUYS FINISH LAST

It is capable of being presented as a discipline, capable of being learned, capable of being practiced. Entrepreneurs need to search purposefully for the sources of innovation, the changes and their symptoms that indicate opportunities for successful innovation. And they need to know and to apply the principles of successful innovation.

Entrepreneurship is not a personality trait. In 30 years I have seen people of the most diverse personalities and temperaments perform well in entrepreneurial challenges. To be sure, people who need certainty are unlikely to make good ntrepreneurs.

Anyone who can face up to decision-making can learn to be an entrepreneur and to behave entrepreneurially. Entrepreneurship then, is behavior rather than personality trait. And its fundation lies in concept and theory rather than in intuition.

HOW TO BECOME A SUCCESSFUL ENTREPRENEUR

SELF EVALUATION

(CIRCLE MOST APPROPRIATE)

Attributes	How I See Myself	How Friends See Me
a. Self-Starter	1 2 3 4 5 6 7 8 9 10	1 2 3 4 5 6 7 8 9 10
b. Born Leader	1 2 3 4 5 6 7 8 9 10	1 2 3 4 5 6 7 8 9 10
c. Well Organized	12 3 4 5 6 7 8 9 10	1 2 3 4 5 6 7 8 9 10
d. Manage People	1 2 3 4 5 6 7 8 9 10	1 2 3 4 5 6 7 8 9 10
e. Creativity	1 2 3 4 5 6 7 8 9 10	1 2 3 4 5 6 7 8 9 10
f. Ingenuity	1 2 3 4 5 6 7 8 9 10	1 2 3 4 5 6 7 8 9 10
g. Commitment	1 2 3 4 5 6 7 8 9 10	1 2 3 4 5 6 7 8 9 10
h. Perserverance	1 2 3 4 5 6 7 8 9 10	1 2 3 4 5 6 7 8 9 10
i. Will Sacrifice	1 2 3 4 5 6 7 8 9 10	1 2 3 4 5 6 7 8 9 10
j. Marketing	1 2 3 4 5 6 7 8 9 10	1 2 3 4 5 6 7 8 9 10
k Sales Ability	1 2 3 4 5 6 7 8 9 10	1 2 3 4 5 6 7 8 9 19
l. Street Smarts	1 2 3 4 5 6 7 8 9 10	1 2 3 4 5 6 7 8 9 10
m. Hard Worker	1 2 3 4 5 6 7 8 9 10	1 2 3 4 5 6 7 8 9 10

Total both sides   ____   __

CHAPTER EIGHT $\quad \lceil$

LEGAL AND TAX STRUCTURE

How to Begin the New Venture. Basic Requirements. Legal And Tax Structures. Single Tax Entities - Sole Proprietor, General Partnership, Limited Partnership. S-Corporation, Limited Liability Company, (LLC), Trusts. Double Tax Entities - C-Corporation, The Nevada Corporation. Other Legal Entities - The Family Limited Partnership.

How to Begin the New Venture

Characteristics of an entrepreneurial venture are: (1) need is identified, (2) a product or service market niche is evaluated and validated, and (3) *added value* is created in a new or existing enterprise. Starting a business where new value is added is almost always entrepreneurial. Acquiring a retail business with an existing customer base where it is difficult to add value (travel agency, automotive repair shop, quick-copy store, flower shop, etc.) may or not meet the criteria for entrepreneurship. It is rarely possible to create new markets or devise new products or service applications in such entities. Little new value is created. Sales may increase due to a new management style and personality or better use of resources, and more creative advertising, but the basic business entity remains the same.

Basic Requirements

Those starting a new business need to know certain basic requirements including:

a. Location for the new business.
b. Applicable city, county, state, and federal laws and regulations.
c. Business tools: profit-and-loss, cash flow projections and business plans.
d. Computer literacy as to word processing and spread-sheets.
e. Presentation and communication skills.
f. Ability to envision alternate products or services.
g. Ability to turn adverse situations to advantage.
h. Nearly every business is inadequately financed; the key is to maximize available resources.
i. A product or service must be timely and viable as determined by the available market.

Legal amd Tax Structures

There are several legal structures available to the new venture: Sole Proprietorship, General Partnership (GP), Limited Partnership (LLP), Subchapter S Corporation (S-Corp), Standard C Corporation (C-Corp) with or without *1244 Election*, Limited Liability Company (LLC), and various types of Trusts. These structures vary from restrictive to flexible, with creative alternatives. Several are convertible to one or more of the other legal forms under certain circumstances, subject to specific restrictions. Others are closed-end, in that they cannot be easily be converted or transferred into another legal entity.

What might be the best legal form in the initial or start-up phase of the business may not necessarily be the most beneficial in subsequent stages of the enterprise. The entrepreneur should obtain information and recommendations in review with a qualified attorney and/or CPA. The following is a thumbnail sketch of each of these legal structure options.

Single Tax Entities
Sole Proprietor

This is basically the owner conducting business in his or her name or in a *dba (doing-business-as)* or *aka (also-known-as)* fictitious name. The individual owner reports annual net income on the IRS 1040 personal income tax form for the taxable (usually calendar) year.

In general, the liabilities of the business are also personal liabilities, since the owner and the business are viewed as the same entity for tax purposes.

To begin doing business as a sole proprietor, it is necessary to obtain applicable occupational licenses (city, county and state) and to register a fictitious name, if used. *Advantages:* modest start-up expense and exemption from certain tax levies and payroll additions. Losses are deductible. *Disadvantages:* high direct and indirect liability exposure to the individual and difficulty in obtaining health and benefit plans.

General Partnership

Two or more individuals enter in general partnership. The requirements of this single tax business form are essentially the same as those listed under the Sole Proprietorship. A fictitious name may be selected and registered with the state (*dba* or *aka*). The taxable period is usually the calendar year. Occupational licenses are required. *Advantages:* Partnership net income is taxed only once and is filed on IRS 1040 personal tax form. Modest start-up expense and exemption from certain tax levies and payroll additions.

Losses are deductible pro-rata to partnership interest. *Disadvantages:* High direct and indirect liability exposure to the individual partners and difficulty in obtaining health and benefit plans.

Though a written agreement is not required by law, it is recommended that partners execute a partnership agreement prior to the initial *honeymoon* period. Basic areas of possible misunderstanding should be addressed, such as which partner will make the final business decisions in case of deadlock; the rights, duties and responsibilities of each individual; and a termination and exit clause. Partnerships don't always operate smoothly or, if they do, people or situations may change, so a buy-sell agreement is recommended. This is an offer made by one partner to buy the other partner's interest which, if not accepted within a reasonable period of time (30 days is often specified), requires that the offeree buy the first partner's interest on the same basis.

There is an inherent difficulty in maintaining a good working relationship. Partnerships tend to be strained if there are substantially higher profits than projected or, conversely, if the business suffers continuing losses.

In the former, the *greed button* often clicks on in one or both partners, leading to intense maneuvering to carve out a larger share. In the latter, family financial pressures may become intolerable and adversely affect the partnership (Susie cannot attend private school, etc.).

Limited Partnership

The Limited Partnership requires a formal written partnership agreement and filing of certificate of limited partnership with the state. There are statutory formalities. One or more general partners have the management responsibility, and liability extends to their personal assets. It is possible for a corporation to serve as the general partner, thus limiting individual liability.

Limited partners are not permitted to take active part in the management of the partnership. As a general rule, the limited partner's actual investment (plus appreciation) and commitments in the partnership agreement, vis-a-vis future investment contributions, are subject to attack by business creditors, but not their personal assets. The Limited Partnership is governed by complex regulations and laws.

S-Corporation

In the S Corporation, also known as the 'S-Corp' or *Subchapter S Corporation*, only one class of common voting stock is authorized, but the corporation may sell bonds. The number of shareholders cannot exceed 75. Annual net earnings or losses pass through to individual shareholders who enjoy limited liability in the corporation. Shares may be transferred, bought and sold. It is often beneficial to prepare a careful Shareholder Agreement with buy-sell and right-of-first-refusal provisions. Whether income is distributed or not, income tax is payable pro-rata to each stockholder's interest at the end of the fiscal year, which is usually the calendar year. Similarly, losses are deductible by shareholders.

For *S-Corporation election,* all shareholders must sign IRS form 2553 on or before the 15th day of the 3rd month of the tax year. (By March 15th if a calendar year). Additional requirements are: only individuals, estates and certain trusts may own *S-Corporation* stock. Voting rights within the single authorized class of stock may vary, as provided in the By-Laws. Some shares, for example, may have no voting rights. An *S-Corp* may not own subsidiaries. *S-Corp* status may be terminated by more than 50 percent vote of the issued and outstanding shares. The corporation will then be taxed as a C-Corp. To re-elect S-Corp status, a period of 5 years must have elapsed. Where heavy start-up losses are incurred, an S Corporation is a good choice because it permits losses to be personally deductible (pro-rata to ownership) by individual shareholders.

Limited Liability Company (LLC)

A relatively new legal structure is the Limited Liability Company (LLC). It is now available in all states. It is a non-incorporated single tax entity with the tax characteristics of a partnership, but with the limited liability of a corporation. There may be more owners than in an *S-Corp*, and any or all of them may be active in management.

There is a limitation on an owner's ability to withdraw from the company and it cannot qualify for Section 1244 ordinary loss provision. An LLC does not automatically qualify in every state for tax treatment as a partnership. In order not to be taxed as an association, the LLC should have limited life (30 years in some states), and not permit free transfer of ownership interests. There are advantages in selecting this structure. i,e, for those who dislike the onerous task of writing at least one set of annual Minutes. The LLC organization which calls for the Owner to be the Manager, does not require that Minutes be prepared,

Trusts

Certain types of trusts are qualified to own businesses. Among these are 'standard' revocable or irrevocable trusts, and irrevocable complex trusts organized by private contractual agreement. In the latter, a Trust Indenture (Declaration of Trust) is prepared by the Grantor/Creator and assets are irrevocably conveyed to the Trust. Typically, the life of this trust is 25 years or more. Trustees are charged with protection of the Corpus (conveyed assets). Beneficiaries of the trust pay personal income taxes on distributions made at the discretion of the trustees and may not be active in trust management. Such trusts may be utilized together with private foundations. Federal reporting is on IRS 1041 and K-1 forms. In general, privacy is enhanced and the assets of the trust are less subject to business creditor liens or attacks. This type of trust requires detailed minutes and record keeping. Due to income tax avoidance abuses in this area, the irrevocable complex trust system is under increasing scrutiny by the IRS.

Double-Tax Entities

C - Corporation

The standard 'C' Corporation is taxed on its net annual income. After-tax income, when distributed to shareholders as dividends, is also taxable. That makes this structure the prime *double-tax* vehicle, beloved by the IRS. Maximum corporate tax rates apply -- usually in the 34 to 39 percent range. Dividends are taxed as personal income. Alternate minimum tax (AMT) additions apply at certain income levels.

Several classes of stock may be authorized and a number of variations selected in a *C-Corp,* as long as they are provided for in the corporate By-Laws or in the amendments thereto. It is often beneficial to make a *1244 election,* i.e., qualify the *C-Corp's* stock as small business stock under Section 1244. Up to $50,000 of losses are recognized as ordinary losses, which are almost always deductible in full. This section was introduced by the provisions of the Omnibus Reconciliation Act of 1993, to induce investors to acquire stock in existing small businesses or start-up ventures. Non-corporate taxpayers may exclude up to 50 percent of the gain they realize on the sale of small business stock issued to them after August 10, 1993, and held for a minimum of 5 years. Total annual sales of the *C-Corp* may not exceed $50 million for this election to apply. Specific limitations govern the amount of the excluded gain and the qualifying trades or businesses.

The structure of the *C-Corp* lends itself to creative applications and various combinations of authorized stock. There can be Class A, Class B, Class C stock or Preferred Stock. Class A might be *organizer stock* issued to the creators of the Company at a nominal cost per share. Class B might be *investor stock* at the offering price per share. Class C could be non-voting, but income-participating stock, etc. There are almost infinite variations. For instance, Preferred Stock may be either a specific kind of voting stock, or a non-voting, non-equity participating stock with guaranteed rate of interest and redemption premium.

Advantages to *C-Corp* structuring include opportunities for *debt instruments with convertibility* into one or another class of stock (such as convertible debentures), loans with equity kickers, warrants, options, and other devices. Blocking rights, anti-dilution, non-assessable clauses, etc. are some of the protection devices against the *Bad Guys*.

Whatever the mix of classes of stock and their restrictions, they should be specified in detail in the corporate By-Laws and preferably in a carefully written Shareholder Agreement, executed by all shareholders with voting rights.

> **Rule.** Again, it is important to use the services of competent certified accountants and attorney in the organizational stages of NEWCO.

Changes in federal, state and local tax laws may require annual review and perfecting, or even changing, the legal and tax structure of the new company.

The Nevada Corporation

For those selecting a *C-Corporation* as their preferred legal structure, there are the traditional alternatives for incorporation: in the state in which the principal incorporator resides; in one of the handful of states which have no state income tax, such as Florida and Wyoming; in the ubiquitous Delaware corporation; or in the Nevada corporation. And, for some entities, offshore corporate registration may be an option.

Please note that the Nevada Secretary of State Office requires that there be a President, Secretary, Treasurer and one Director stated in the incorporating documents. There may be only one person in all the offices. Thus virtually any person could be elected President, Secretary and Treasurer. (It may be anecdotal, but in one case, a homeless person and in another a mother-in-law, were supposedly elected Presidents of such companies.)

In a Nevada Corporation, one or more Vice Presidents could be elected (yet not be disclosed) and be given all the powers and control normally reserved for the President of the corporation. This provides a high degree of personal protection and privacy. Another advantage is shareholder privacy. The incorporator is not required to submit a list of stockholders when filing for a new corporation, since Nevada requires no official list of corporate shareholders.

Liberal stock ownership is a fact of life. *Bearer stock* is authorized. It is also possible to operate multiple businesses within the same corporation. Another bonus is the fact that so far Nevada is reportedly the only state which has *no information sharing agreement* with the IRS. Any attorney embarking on a fishing expedition to identify assets in a Nevada corporation might find it a frustrating experience.

And, a word to the wise, there is a higher per capita IRS audit rate of Nevada corporations than in other states.

Other Legal Entities

The Family Limited Partnership

Application is made for a *Family Limited Partnership* by filing with IRS for a Federal Tax Identification number (EIN) using form IRS Form SS-4. One of many creative approaches to be considered.

Example: Mother and Dad, General Partners acquire 5 percent ownership each, the children as Limited Partners receive the remaining 90 percent. The *Family Limited Partnership* is a pass-through entity, and limited partners receive unearned income. Thus no FICA is due, resulting in savings as high as 15.3 percent on the applicable income. There is flexibility in the manner in which the *Family Limited Partnership* can be organized.

General Partners may provide that income not be distributed annually on a pro-rata basis to ownership of partnership interests, but held for future distribution. Of course, income taxes must be paid annually pro-rata on the childrens' interest in the limited partnership at their lower tax rate. This structure may permit savings in FICA and income taxes.

> **Rule** *There must be a bona fide business operation in The Family Limited Partnership or it may be disallowed by the Internal Revenue Service.*

.

CHAPTER NINE []

THE BAD GUYS -THEIR METHODS - HOW TO MAKE THEM FINISH LAST

The "Bump and Run"- Shares of Common Voting Stock, Shares of Common Voting Stock Fully-Paid and Non-Assessable - Personal garantees and "Triggers" Are Unacceptable in Bank Loans, Never "Secure" your accounts payable, How to Obtain Best Credit Terms for NEWCO.

T he "Bump-and-Run"
It's not uncommon for an inventor-entrepreneur to be initially successful --- too successful.

Suddenly and — to the owner — unexpectedly, positive cash flow falters. It is a challenge to meet payroll, withholding, and social security taxes, and other business obligations. The entrepreneur is confused, not realizing that the business has become *too successful*.   He or she is unaware of the unforgiving business rule-of-thumb that says that, as a minimum, 15 percent of net annual sales will be required in working capital just to service accounts receivable. Also, two months inventory of materials and factory supplies plus 25 percent of sales in the case of the new company (let's call it NEWCO) requires additional operating funds. This does not include outlays for the acquisition of new machinery, equipment maintenance, research and development, etc.

To cover this negative cash flow situation, the inventor-entrepreneur visits a banker with profit-and-loss and cash flow projection spreadsheets in hand or, more often than not, with only an independent accountant's Operating and Financial Statements. Business prospects are bright. But the bank is not interested in providing a loan, due to insufficient collateral.

The entrepreneur is forced to seek investors. Obsessed with retaining control of the company, he or she is unable to attract substantial funds. Nights are sleepless, the business precarious.

Enter the *Bump-and-Run* investor, who calms and reassures the inventor-entrepreneur; offers to invest whatever amounts of capital are needed, taking only a minority interest. Both parties agree that since the company is only two years old, the market value of the business is three times (instead of perhaps five times or more) the average annual earnings before taxes. The value of the company is set at $1 million at the insistence of the owner.

The investor says,

"We are willing to back you and invest whatever your company needs. Our stock interest will be pro-rata based on the value which you set for the company. Please ask for all you will need, because if you come to us later for additional funds, it will be a *different conversation*."

The owner doesn't hear, or at least pays no attention, to the warning. He is preoccupied with the desire to limit the amount of outside ownership, and to prove to the outside investor that he can manage the business with the least possible additional capital. Even though projections indicate a minimum of $400,000 will be needed, the inventor-entrepreneur believes $300,000 will suffice.

"All right, according to the agreed formula, for an investment of $300,000, I will sell you a 30 percent common voting stock interest in the Company."

"Good. You have our commitment to invest $300,000 for 30 percent of the common voting stock of the company. Now, are you *sure* this is enough for your ongoing capital needs?"

The answer is in the affirmative.

"Remember, it is important that you understand that if you need more investment later on, there will be a different conversation. If you need more capital now, just say so."

The investor has put the entrepreneur on notice.

The *Bump* is completed. With the investor's backing and contacts, the business continues to prosper, and sales soar to 2 million dollars in the third year. Once again, cash flow is tight. The inventor-entrepreneur requests an urgent meeting with the investor, confident that the additional funds will be supplied.

"Mr. Investor, we have been doing splendidly! Profits are far beyond our projections due to increased sales and the improved management and controls provided by your people. But we now need an additional $500,000."

After a meaningful pause, the investor replies,

"Let me refer you to our original deal. You were told, not once but several times, to ask us at that time for all the investment you would *ever* need. Otherwise, we would have to reconsider. Now, we cannot make a further investment unless we have a controlling interest."

The *Run* is now in place.

At this point, the inventor-entrepreneur exclaims angrily,

"I'd rather see the company fail than give up controlling interest. So, I'll just bankrupt it!"

The investor replies,

"You do what you have to do. We are prepared to lose the funds invested. But don't make a decision now. "We are in no hurry. Let us know your plans."

The inventor pours his heart out to his wife that night as he paces the floor. He proclaims again and again how he will just let the business go under. She listens and assures him of her complete support, whatever he decides to do. Across town, the investor sleeps well, confident that the inventor's love for his creation will not permit him to file for bankruptcy protection.

A few days later a subdued entrepreneur meets with the investor. The value of the stock is updated to include earnings of the third year of operations. The $500,000 is paid in and the investor is issued additional shares of common voting stock equivalent to 60 percent of the company, leaving the inventor with 40 percent total interest. Additional key management and technical people are brought into the firm and the original owner is rarely consulted.

The business prospers and the following year again requires additional working capital. The investor notifies the inventor that an additional $500,000 is needed and that his pro-rata share is $200,000.

"But, I don't have that kind of money!"

"If you can't come up with your pro-rata share of the new funds, we will have to purchase additional shares and dilute your interest accordingly."

And so it goes. A year or so later, the original owner's interest is less than 10 percent, a small slice of the big pie. At some point the entrepreneur decides — or is pressured — to sell the remaining interest to the investor, often receiving enough to live comfortably the rest of his or her life. This settlement is not due to any generosity on the part of the investor, but comes from an awareness that a belligerent and persistent minority shareholder can be a significant detriment.

And so the inventor-entrepreneur, who would have endangered his very life to protect his 'baby', is finally divested of all he holds dear. In his bitterness he tells anyone who will listen how: "Those *!%?!!* investors stole my company!"

Fortunately, there are valid ways to protect against the *Bump-and-Run* strategy and make the Bad Guys — in this case the investors — finish last, or at least not ahead of the entrepreneur.

Shares of Common Voting Stock Fully-Paid and Non-Assesable.

My recommendation is that the entrepreneur include somewhere in the Agreement with the *Bump and Run investor,* the following language,

"It is understood and mutually agreed that 25% of the shares of common voting stock owned by the entrepreneur *are fully paid and non assessable.".*

*This ensures that the entrepreneu*r is secured in a minority interest, no matter what happens. The investor, in his or her optimism. often ignores such a clause

Personal Guarantees and "Triggers"Are Unacceptable in Bank Loans

In the first meetings with the loan officer enough questions need to be asked to determine the 'origination costs' of the loan or line of credit -- both published and hidden. Loan documents must be studied carefully for things like commitment fees, discounted interest in advance, lags in check clearances (the bank uses the client's money during 'check-clearing float time', and 'holds'), prepayment penalties, etc.

In addition, banks are fond of inserting 'triggers' or contingencies into loan documents, which place an undue burden on the owner in both capital cost and bookkeeping. Some of these contingencies are: a compensating balance requirement (a minimum amount of funds on deposit), no decrease in net worth, no decrease in working capital, failure to keep a certain debt-asset ratio, and many more. Any one of these triggers can automatically place the loan in default, subject to immediate call by the bank, even though payments are being met on time and the loan serviced in a satisfactory manner.

Make it clear in the first conversation *that triggers are unacceptable* -- a marvelous word for the use of entrepreneurs -- that the only acceptable contingencies in the loan documents are failure to make loan interest and principal payments in a timely fashion. If the banker insists on triggers, find another banking relationship.

Bankers refer, in their approval process, to certain ratios on financial statements, many of which are important control items for the entrepreneur. 'Inventory Turnover' refers to the number of times inventory is sold and replaced during the fiscal year. 'Accounts Receivable Collection Days' are calculated in a formula in which the total of Accounts Receivable is divided by sales, then multiplied by days in the period (usually one month). 'Receivable Turnover' equals Net Sales divided by average Accounts Receivable, etc. For an excellent reference on this subject, refer to Chapter 6 of The Ernst & Young's Guide to Financing for Growth, by Daniel R. Garner and published by John Wiley & Sons (1994).

Banking relationships with entrepreneurs are often ephemeral because of the mercurial nature of new businesses. An apparent cordial understanding, even friendship, with the banker, will all-too-quickly cool if the new business does not meet (for whatever reason) its projections. And, if worsening ratios appear on financial statements -- perhaps heralding temporary financial adversity

-- the bank may, without warning, move from a position of support and financial backing to one of positioning to grab assets. Then the 'friendly banker' may become one of the Bad Guys with whom one has to be prepared to do battle.

Never "Secure" Your Accounts Payable

Some credit managers of vendors ask that you secure the accounts payable, i.e., the amount you owe them for materials, purchase parts, factory supplies, etc. A few even request a personal or corporate promissory note for your purchases. They will usually desist from their demands upon your calm, but firm, statement that any request for any security beyond the promise to pay the account payable on or before its due date, is *unacceptable*.

Often overlooked -- but important to the positive cash flow of the new entity -- is the value of extended credit from principal vendors. In today's vernacular, 'it doesn't take a rocket scientist' to understand that if receivables are collected within 30 to 45 days of billing and vendors paid at 45 to 60 days, thousands of dollars of positive cash flow will be achieved. When principal vendors agree to approve extended credit terms, they become, in effect, short-term, interest-free lenders.

When approaching the vendor, it is well to keep in mind that, due to their bad experience with NEWCOS (their high mortality rate and the resultant collection hassles) the credit department has to exercise caution with start-ups. But if there is a reasonable assurance of credit compliance, credit officers will usually authorize favorable credit terms -- mainly because they are also under constant pressure to enable their company to achieve higher sales and profits.

How to Obtain Best Credit Terms for NEWCO.

1. Meet personally with the vendor's credit officer (or other decision-maker). Review with him or her the Company's business plan, its projected profitability and growth prospects.

2. Project confidence and ability. Develop a climate of sincerity and trust. Remember, the credit officer wants your business if the credit risk seems acceptable.

3. Emphasize that, as the vendor helps the fledgling new business with extended terms of credit, a preferred prime vendor relationship will be created which will continue as the company grows.

4. Request approval of a revolving credit line at 45, 60 or even a 90 days terms-of-payment schedule, depending on the indications of what the vendor might approve. Be prepared for objections such as, "We are not bankers." Acknowledge their concern and continue the presentation.

5. Be prepared for vendor approval of half or less of the requested revolving extended-terms credit limit on a trial basis. After a favorable payment history, over several purchase and payment cycles, the vendor will usually approve increases in the credit line. If one vendor declines to grant advantageous credit terms, contact its competitors.

CHAPTER TEN

BUILDING TOWARD YOUR EXIT PLAN

Building Toward Your Exit Plan. Deferred Compensation. Deferred Compliance with Social Levies. The Five Basic Types of Exit Plans: Building Block Exit Plan. Exit by Succession. Exit by Capitalization. Exit by IPO. Exit Plan by Strategy. The First Line of Defense.

Quite often, the eldest sons (and daughters) of entrepreneurial fathers and/or grandfathers (sometimes skipping a generation) follow in their footsteps. If the predecessors were cautious and stayed free of debt; built the enterprise carefully,and conservatively to create asset value, with a view to capitalizing, their descendants often renewed the cycle.

Like their ancestors, they leave the growing and polishing of the business to professional managers. Studies show that by age 55 entrepreneurial creator-innovators originate 5 different ventures in their lifetime.

Apparently, the energies, enthusiasm and dedication which are the mark of 'young Turk' entrepreneurs flag considerably by then. There are, of course, exceptions. I have met indefatigable septuagenarians fully involved in creating more than double that number of entities.

As for myself, I have completed my allotted five ventures (and more) from inception to capitalization. I am still open to new opportunities, but only if they meet the following criteria:

- No more than three employees.
- Semi-automatic or automatic molded or manufactured sub-assemblies.
- Assembly of products designed for sale to stocking distributors.
- Net profits of at least 15 to 30 percent of sales.

> **Rule**. *In the absence of a valid exit strategy, events will inexorably dictate the final exit plan for the business.*

Building Toward Your Exit Plan

One characteristic of entrepreneurs is that they almost always have a valid exit plan--selected in the initial planning stage -- which reflects the creator's purpose, needs, beliefs, background and persona.

Exit plans may be as varied as each venturer's needs and purposes. In the absence of an Exit Plan, it is probable that an involuntary exit will be enforced by any of a number of circumstances: loss of market, competition, a better mousetrap, changes in customer acceptance, inept management, catering to wants instead of needs, lack of cost controls, etc.

It is a proven fact that only a small percentage (1 of 10) of businesses survive the first year of operations. Many more fall out -- unless able to adjust the mix of products and services to changing markets -- during the first 5 years, dubbed the *half-life* of a business. A minority of companies continue in a growth pattern beyond 10 years. I recently noted in a yellowed printed program announcing a world-wide church conference in 1932, that less than 10 percent of local advertisers had survived.

Entrepreneurial ventures fare considerably better than the norm because, in general, they are founded on more careful analysis and research as to market niche, viability of product or services, etc. All possible risk is usually eliminated in the start-up phase. As previously stated, entrepreneurs are not risk-takers.

Deferred Compensation

No owner takes anything out of NEWCO until the financial situation warrants, as determined by the Board of Directors. I suggest that the business initially operate under a policy of *deferred compensation*, in which each owner sends in a monthly *pro-forma* (dummy) invoice for work performed, at an agreed rate of compensaation (In my case $20 per hour). When the Company situation permited, the owner pro-forma invoices are approved in sequence for payment by NEWCO. In the meantime the owner invoices are not booked.,

Deferred Compliance with Social Levies

This, coupled with *deferred compliance* with social levies(social security, workmen compensation. etc.) minimizes the costs of administration, There is minimal institutional debt, resulting in a higher level of annual profits, so that the standard multiplier in an Exit Plan should ultimately result in a higher selling price for the stock or assets, and a higher than normal (5 to 8 times earnings), and a healthy return on investment (ROI). The compliance with social levies may (or not) coincide with payment of the owners pro-forma invoices.

This procedure was followed at *Vu-Flow Filters Company,* starting with $6.000 total paid-in capital, plus a one-time bank loan of $10.000, repaid in six months. This yielded a total of $750.000 in a sale of assets six years later, and payment of *previous invoices* by the owners -- *deferred compensation* -- of total salaries to the three owners each year, during the last three years of their ownership. The ROI is astronomical.

Five Basic Types of Exit Plans
Building Block Exit Plan

Some entrepreneurs envision their Exit Plan of ongoing 'building block' activity, broadening -- through acquisition and innovation -- new and complementary markets. They often seek financing in the public market. Bill Gates and Microsoft are the most visible leaders of this strategy. Their plan to exit is through control of new markets and accelerated growth.

Exit by Succession

Others continue to expand the company with new products and services, adjusting marketing strategies along the way. The Exit Plan is one of succession, the transfer of control from father to son. J. Willard Marriott and his humble beginnings with one Hot Shoppe is one example.

Exit by Capitalizaion

The Exit Plan most often utilized by those entrepreneurs who work with OPM and quit their *day jobs* to devote full-time to the new business, and have no choice but to support their basic standard of living from their resources and borrowed capital. They typically mortgage their homes to the hilt, cajole family and friends for loans, aggressively seek investors, etc.

As the business grows, interim bank financing is a must. Rarely do these entrerprises attract the attention of venture capital sources, nor do they 'go public' with an IPO. If the project fails, the resultant debris is awesome. If it succeeds all the players may benefit.

Those who initiate the new venture with minimal personal capital rely on income from employment, fees, or other sources to meet their family's monthly expenses. They rarely accept loans from others, and take nothing -- often not even reimbursable expenses -- out of the company in the first or second stage of growth. With minimal administrative costs, they are able to build the business rapidly with far less capital. This is the domain of sweat equity.

Exit by IPO.

Hard-driving men and women typically organize a business and ramp it up from stage to stage, culminating in an *Initial Public Offering* (IPO). Though they may maintain a minority position in the public company, their main thrust is to create a new company with capital acquired from an IPO, and move it along the same path as the first venture.

They may do this again and again. Some speak of a *life of terror* because of the inherent pressures and personal financial exposure along the way. .

Exit Plan by Strategy.

Business owners in need of capital to build the company for the long-pull, should, as was noted in previous chapters, avoid the *Bump-and-Run investors*. Such people are creator/ implementers for their own Exit Plan.

But there is an exception. The *Bump-and-Run investor* can be beneficial to the entrepreneur who plans an orderly exit to capitalize. Why? Because the goal of both parties is the same. That is, for the entrepreneur's interest to pass to the investor. It then becomes a matter of *when* that takes place and *for how much*.

We have noted in the previous chapter that there are ways to make such Bad Guy investors become Good Guys in spite of themselves. Because of their nearly 100 percent success rate in lucrative takeovers, *Bump-and-Run investors* tend to believe they are infallible. Therefore, it is possible for the owner of the targeted enterprise to insist on non-negotiable items as part of the initial funding agreement.

The First Line of Defense

The first line of defense is possible due to the optimism of the *Bump and Run Investor* The owner inserts in the first draft of the inital agreement words similar to these: "25% of the Company's common voting stock now owned by (Name of the Owner) is hereby deemed to be fully paid and non-assessable". When the B&R investor decides it is time to dilute the owner's interest he finds that his dilution by issuing stock for additional investment dilutes the owner, but only to the threshold of one quarter of the issued and outstanding stock of the Company,

CHAPTER ELEVEN

BAD GUYS VS. GOOD GUYS

The Mid-Career Entrepreneur. Humphrey Associates, Inc. The Conclusion. Dangers of "Holding On". The Designer-Entrepreneur. Hectore Manufacturing Inc. Never Accept an Office in an Unknown Company. Read Every File in the Company. How to Make Bad Guy Investors Finish Last. The Little Yellow Dog. Air Compak Freight Forwarders. Inc. The Villager Condominium. Winning a Struggle Against Lender Bad Guys. How to Keep a Good Guy Investor from Being a Bad Guy. Conclusion.

The *Mid-Career Entrepreneur,* Enterprise Dearborn (1993), Joseph R. Mancuso outlines thoroughly how to successfully acquire a business. He has developed *The Search* almost into an art form.

There are usually more Buyers than there are Sellers. It is not uncommon for investor friends of mine to call me to see if I know of a business they might buy. My reply is nearly always,

"Hey, if I knew of a good business for sale at a reasonable price, *I'd* buy it."

Unless deeply motivated, Sellers tend to overestimate their companies' value. If a Buyer has to look forward, after purchasing a company, to 8 or 10 years of profitable operations to recapture their investment, it may be unrewarding.

For favorable leverage and a payout in less than 5 years, look for troubled companies with inherent potential, but which suffer from lack of management, mismanagement, or financial anemia. Of course there must also be a motivated Seller.

And, though not for the faint-hearted, there are companies in shambles, one step away from Federal Bankruptcy Court, which can be rescued through heroic effort. Lastly, there are companies already under the protection of one or another of the federal bankruptcy laws, which might be attractive to a Buyer able to walk the company through the tedium of government regulations, in order to bring it to profitability,and out of bankruptcy.

The age and condition of the target company being acquired largely determines the number of challenges and contingencies which, unless identified and neutralized, might *fleece* the new owner.

At one extreme is the first type of entity noted above--probably overpriced-- but with business affairs in good order. At the other extreme is the floundering, failing company, in various stages of disarray. The latter harbors not only contingencies, but costly surprises (intended or not) which require that the Buyer be vigilant.

> **Rule**. *The older the company, the worse its condition, the more debris it accumulates, such as disputes, pending litigation, claims, etc. In buying such a company or its assets, allow a substantial 'fudge factor', a financial buffer for such contingencies.*

Humphrey Associates, Inc.

I acquired a custom furniture manufacturing company with a minimal positive net worth from three of my friends..they were all good businessmen The company had previously failed due to mismanagement. However, with the *law of the next optimist* at work, new investors came forward, but soon found their investment endangered with the same (mis)management. Projections indicated that by careful management, changes in product mix and aggressive marketing, it would become viable. but it would require considerable effort. Due to the precarious situation of the firm, I structured the purchase of all the issued and outstanding stock on an option basis, so that I could cut my losses if unforeseen events prevented me from turning the company around. This was my fudge factor, my 'out' if everything turned to mud.

Dorothy, as my accountant, asked the President for the corporate books. He pointed to a box. There were records all right; three sets of books, each one a different bookkeeping system, which had been posted for a few months, then abandoned. I had personally taken a physical inventory, but had not personally verified the accounts receivable, which was a mistake.

I telephoned a customer, a friend of mine, who had been invoiced for custom mahogany desks.

"When can we expect payment?"

"What do you mean? The desks haven't been delivered yet."

I showed the invoice to the former CEO. He stood

hipshot, squinting one eye against ubiquitous cigarette smoke as it curled upward. I asked if the desks were ready for delivery.

"No, they aren't manufactured yet." He continued,

"You see, in order to avoid a 'swing' in sales from month to month, we *'pre-invoice'* make the monthly sales curve more uniform."

Now *that* was an original concept!

"Uh. How many other pre-invoices are there?"

The telephone interrupted our interesting conversation before he could reply. It was a vendor who wanted to know when his invoice would be paid.

"Dave, this invoice is not on the list of certified payables you gave me at closing," I said,

"Uh," again a thoughtful squint. "Guess I forgot it."

Every few days someone else called to request payment, with the same response,

"Guess I forgot it."

A few months later, one of the former owners, a leading attorney, called to tell me that I owed more than 12 months unpaid rent on the factory building, and that it had to be paid or he would have to take legal action. Though I protested that this obligation was not included in our purchase agreement, he was adamant.

The Conclusion

The situation called for firm, creative action. The facts:

1. There was no longer a positive but a *minus* net worth due to 'pre-invoicing' of several large orders -- which meant the *sale* had been recorded, but no costs against it; no materials, labor, or general and administrative expenses (G&A).

2. There were several thousand dollars of additional "Guess-I-forgot-it" accounts payable.

3. And, a former owner planned to take over the business by legal action unless I paid   a year's back rent.

I called my employees together and informed them that Mr. Orebsteib, who owned the factory building, planned to try to take over the company, and that, as they knew, he had full-time guards watching the property to keep us from moving.

"If we're going to save the business, and your jobs, I'll need your help. I've rented space in a better location and installed wiring for the machinery and equipment. Tomorrow is Thanksgiving Day. The Owner will be enjoying his turkey dinner and the guards will have the day off. I can't afford to pay you anything now to move the company. How many are willing to come early tomorrow morning?"

They all raised their hands.

Shortly after dawn the following day a big van quietly backed to the factory loading dock. By late morning it was loaded and the building stripped, including the wiring. We installed the machinery and equipment at the new location with "quick-connect" plugs and were in operation the following Monday morning. The telephone rang.

"Gardner, what do you think you're doing?"

"We needed a better location for the factory. Didn't I tell you?"

"I have the same remedy, regardless of your move."

"That's right. Come and get the keys."

Silence. He knew it would cost many thousands of dollars to re-wire and install the factory at its old location.

I continued,

"Though the unpaid rent you claim was not part of our deal, to show good faith I am willing to give you 24 pro-rata postdated monthly checks -- no interest -- for the full amount."

I enjoyed seeing the cancelled check arrive with each monthly bank statement. The attempt to fleece had failed.

Months later, he called me.

"Gardner, you are the toughest businessman I know. Let's do a deal together."

"Thanks -- but **yes. I guess not!**"!

When I paid Mr. Oribsteib for his shares of stock a little more than 2 years later, the negotiated amount was considerably less than the option formula and included a deduction for *twice the back rent* he had forced me to pay. He later said, almost plaintively,

"You paid the others more for their stock."

"Because they had faith, I paid the option amount in full... but you didn't.have enough faith in me."

I could have sued the owners and most likely prevailed. However, my personal policy has always been to avoid -- and never initiate -- legal action, but be ready to defend against and win any action brought by others. It is far more profitable to devote energies to the project at hand than to litigate.

Dangers of "Holding On"

An excellent guide which has served me well in my entrepreneurial life is taken from a passage of ancient scriptures.

"There is... a time to keep and a time to cast away." (O.T. Eclesiastes. 5:6).

Yes, there *is* a time to hold onto and a time to sell a business. The ultimate decision should be governed by the potential 'shelf-life' and characteristics of the enterprise, and by the mission and purpose of the owner.

As for me, I have always taken the first profit and never looked back, content to count my *gelt* and move on to the next project. Let the new owners take the venture to new heights and reap the greater reward.

In their optimism, some owners plan to capitalize when the business peaks. That is a lot like trying to predict an upturn or downturn in the stock market. It is manifestly impossible. Others, through inertia or optimism, hold on until the company value has greatly diminished.

> **Rule**. *Implement the exit plan as soon as possible after planned parameters have been met. Don't let either optimism or greed keep it all from 'coming true."*

The Designer-Entrepreneur

Early this year a designer and producer of outerwear asked me to advise him regarding a specific challenge. He shared an experience that took place 2 years ago at what, he now recognizes, was the peak of his company's success. He refused a firm offer of high seven figures for his shares of stock. Not long thereafter unexpected and unforeseen changes, beyond his control, in economic conditions and the market drastically curtailed the business, and the window of opportunity closed.

Hectore Manufacturing, Inc,

Murray Rosson asked me, as a good friend, to look at his Florida business, and gave me full power to act in his name. This Company manufactured Wood Roof Trusses and Wood and Aluminum Factory Buildings in Pensacola, which were Assembled On Site, in Orlando, Florida. There were 20 Shareholders in *Hectore Manufacturing Inc*, mostly Doctors and Dentists.

Also, I monitored *Penterra Company* which invested in the latest deals of its President, Kenneth Alred, buying and selling real estate, wth my client's money in Brevard County, Florida.

I sized up the man I was to replace. I found him to be a crooked attorney. A short man with a ready smile, Larry Jones, by marvelous charm and convincing manner, was able to sell minority interests to the investors in *Hectore Manufacturing Inc*. Upon my arrival. we had to ask for additional capital. The investors were extremely upset, and the phone rang constantly with threats and demands for explanation.

Never Accept an Office in an Unknown Company

Larry was at his charming best. He said that I had been named by the Board of Directors to be President of *Hectore Manufacturing Inc*. I promptly declined the honor in writing, since a President is *personally* liable for unpaid social security and income taxes, and delivered the letter to his office.

> **Rule:** *Never accept a position in a company, such as President, Executive Vice President, or even General Manager, which entails personal liability, without weighing the risks that accompany said position.*

I went in to see Larry,

"I reviewed the financials, and apparently we owe
    $36,000 in Social Security taxes?"

Larry gave me a big smile of reassurance.

"Here's the check stub. The check was mailed last
week,"

"Uh huh, and I am not 'Johnny-off-the-pickle-boat,' I
thought.

Read Every File in the Company -

When the offices closed Friday evening, I began to read
every file and made careful notes of each. Late Sunday
morning I found, in a file drawer tucked away in a folder,
the $36,000 check, the signature torn off.

Monday morning came.

"Larry, here is the $36,000 check to the IRS for
unpaid Social Security taxes. It was never mailed."

He was unperturbed, as most rogues are when caught.

"My secretary made a mistake. I'll take care of it."

After we moved to Satellite Beach, Florida, a year or so
later, I was no longer associated with *Hectore Manufac-turing Inc.* It had been closed down as not being a viable
entity. An IRS field agent arrived at our home to collect
the $36,000 unpaid Social Security levies, plus the fines,
penalties, interest, etc. owed by the truss factory.

"Mr. Russell, we are informed, as President of *Hectore
Manufacturing Inc,* that you are responsible for these un-paid Social Security taxes while you were President of that
company."

My documentation was complete. I had never been Presi-dent. The agent was very angry.

"That man sent me on a wild goose chase. He will pay."

Larry paid the debt personally over a period of years. Here is a rule to keep in mind:

.

> **Rule**. *A title, such as President, Executive Vice President or even General Manager, may entail personal liability for unpaid Federal and State social levies and income tax withholding taxes. When signing as an officer of a company, always include the title immediately after the signature to avoid personal liability*

Hector Manufacturing Inc. was a sobering lesson. If I was ever tempted to accept OPM from professionals, the idea was driven from my mind by this experience.

> **Rule**. *When seeking investors for the long haul, the last people to consider bringing into NEWCO are professionals, such as those in the medical field. They look for an immediate return on their investment. They have, in general, little-- if any--entrepreneurial and basic business skills, and are short* on patience and understanding.

How to Make Bad-Guy Investors Finish Last

In previous chapters we have discussed how to survive the *"Bump-and-Run"* Investor. As a *non-negotiable* item, the entrepreneur insists that 25 percent of the capital voting stock of the company owned by him or her, be *fully paid and non-assessable*. That stock can never be assessed for additional capital or subject to any call for additional funds.

The remaining 75 percent is assessable, pro-rata ownership, and subject to 'calls' for additional capital on a pro-rata basis. The optimum solution for any entrepreneur is to provide start-up and working capital through self-generated seed capital (savings, investments, etc.) and loans to the company by family and friends or purchase of shares of stock by them. Should this prove to be inadequate for ongoing company needs, additional equity or debt funding from third parties becomes a necessity.

The process to pre-qualify an investor was outlined in a previous chapter. If, however, the investor selection was faulty, or the investor changed from Good to Bad Guy, it is possible to make that *Bad Guy Investor* Finish Last.

> **Rule.** *I have found that there is always a way to solve the Good Guy's challenges. It is a matter of being creative, of "thinking outside the box", and being bold and resourceful.*

Winning a Struggle Against an Investor Bad Guy   Not too long ago, a client, who will be called Jones, approached me. He wanted to settle pending litigation. For health reasons, he had sold the common voting shares of stock in the

Holden Company. to his associate Matkowski. The thriving business contracted purchasing services to hospitals, nursing homes, restaurants, etc.

Somehow in his subsequent move to another state, all Jones' purchase documents and files disappeared. The tough-minded associate, Matkowski, a Bad Guy street-fighter type, found an excuse to cease making the stipulated monthly payments.

Prior to engaging my services, Jones, my client, had sued Matkowski for specific performance and was almost immediately served with a counter suit in high five figures. Attorneys were positioned to do battle, fee clocks had started to run. As I reviewed the situation, it was obvious that my client might not prevail in the counter suit because there was no paper trail. I called Matkowski, who at first referred me to his attorney. My suggestion was that it might be beneficial for him to listen unless he enjoyed paying legal fees. We entered into direct negotiations which proved fruitless, because Matkowski was not motivated. I decided it was time to get his attention.

"Mr. Matkowski, I am sorry we could not work something out, because that means there will have to be a *struggle*. And I want you to know that I never lose a *struggle*."

It is important not to use the word *"fight"* since it invites confrontation. *"Struggle"* does not. Sometimes the entrepreneur must have some of the attributes of the *little yellow dog*, in the story below, to make *Bad Guy Investors Finish Last*. I like the story of the "Little Yellow Dog" and commend it to you.

The Little Yellow Dog
A beautiful young lady walked her

*dog every morning. A single man
observed her ugly little yellow dog
on its leash. It occurred to him io
rent a Great Dane, and, indeed, she
stopped to admire him. He essayed,
"What breed of dog is that?" "Before
I tell you, it most importany that you
do not utter the word (she spelled it
out)' f-i-g-h-t', or my dog, he will
kill yours." "You mean that if I say
'fight' your dog will attack mine?" In
an instant the little dog jumped up
and with one bite, killed the Great
Dane. "My, what kind of dog is that?"
"I don't know," she said. "But, before
they cut off its tail and painted it yellow, they called it 'crocodile!'"*

(author unknown)

There are times when each of us has to be a Little Yellow Dog.

Mike (by now we were on a first name basis), you are aware of the Shareholder Agreement which governs the Company's stakeholder interests. You have issued to yourself a large number of shares of the common voting stock of the Company, and in doing so have diluted my client's interest."

"Yes, I know," he said.

"And by doing so, you also diluted a third party minority shareholder to the point where she now owns *less than 10 percent* of the issued and outstanding shares.of common voting stock. Therefore, she is excluded from the restriction in the Buy/Sell agreement which states that,

"Owners of *less than 10 percent* of the shares of the
Company are not bound by the Agreement."

"What's your point?"

"Well, what would you say if I told you that I met with her and found her to be very upset at the dilution. And let's suppose she has agreed to sell her shares to your ex-associate, who appears anxious to own minority shareholder rights in your Company."

There was silence for a long moment.

"What do you propose?" Matkowski asked,

"That you pay my client a lump sum of (and I named the amount), that all litigation be dropped, and mutual releases signed."

We negotiated a final amount and the matter was settled. A few months later Matkowski telephoned me,

"Gardner, I need your help with a problem."

"Yes, I guess not!'

Air Compak Freight Forwarders. Inc.

Tom Wilson owned 50 percent of a large freight forwarding company. My client controlled sales and marketing, the other 50 percent shareholder was responsible for finances and administration. The latter had skimmed at least $250,000 from the company, so there was little cash. An airline had to be paid $750,000 in 10 days.

"Gardner, you have to find me new investors to cover this payment or we are bankrupt!"

I did an in-depth review of the financial situation.

"Tom, there is no need to bring in investors if you will agree to follow my recommendations."

We began an intensive collection effort and convinced major customers to make advance payments. At the same time, I was able to get major airlines to extend credit beyond the standard 10 days, but still had to devise a strategy to delay, for a few days, the large payment due.

I was relieved when a clerk -- not an officer -- called from the airline. I could hear sounds of a Christmas office party in the background. She asked if the check had been sent.

I replied, "We have been waiting for instructions as to where to send the payment, since our main offices have moved to Florida." I could tell she was anxious to rejoin the party.

"Please send the check to our Miami office, not to Tampa, because they would not know what to do with it."

That same day we mailed the check for the full $750,000. to the airlines Tampa office. We were still short $100,000 which -- with a sigh of relief -- I collected 10 days later. As I had hoped, the Tampa manager held the check for 2 weeks awaiting main office instructions. The first critical hurdle had been overcome.

I strongly counselled the owner,

"We have to move all corporate bank accounts from your state to Florida. There is too much money involved, and your associate has too many connections there."

He delayed. My concern mounted.

A telephone call to the bank confirmed my misgivings. "All Company accounts have been frozen by the court," the banker reported. The bank had also been named co-defendant in the lawsuit filed by the adverse stockholder, who claimed my client was squandering the assets of the company. We had not been notified of the lawsuit because our own attorney had conspired with the other stakeholder, to have the funds impounded, then served as our company's registered agent.

Had I not called the bank, the funds in the company accounts would have been placed in court custody. The court clerk assured me that, once the funds were in the court jurisdiction, it would take 6 weeks -- at least -- to get them released. By that time the company would be insolvent. The banker obligingly faxed a copy of the lawsuit.

After studying the complaint for several hours, a strategy dawned. A clause in the complaint stated that frozen funds could be used only to pay legitimate accounts payable. I contacted the airline, which cooperated and provided us with a proper invoice.

The following day, Friday, our attorneys obtained a court order to instruct the bank to issue a cashier's check to the airline for the full amount frozen in the bank account -- $367,000.

We presented the court order an hour before bank closing time, while the adversary shareholder and his (our) attorney were out of town. Bank officers scurried around frantically, and finally had no alternative but to issue a cashier's check, which we delivered to the airline that same day.

Crisis averted, the business prospered. It was not long before the bank balance averaged $1 million dollars. We fought off every legal attempt of the dissident shareholder and ignored his threats. When I travelled to his city to negotiate the final settlement, my success at making another Bad Guy Investor Finish Last was highlighted when he asked, "Aren't you afraid to meet with me, alone?"

In the bright clarity of hindsight, I should have been more concerned. Matkowski had every reason to 'buy me a pair of concrete boots' and make me disappear.!

The Villager Condominium
Winning a Struggle Against a Lender Bad Guy

One of the investments of my client, Mel Jones. was in the first high-rise building in Satellite Beach, Florida. *The Villager.* now 80 percent complete. The lender who financed the construction, was a REIT (Real Estate Investment Trust) from Buffalo, New York. The REIT had been paying construction draws on schedule but now was making excuses, demanding additional information, anything it seemed, to delay payment.

A few telephone calls revealed an alarming trend. Several projects financed by this REIT had been 'taken over' by them, completed and sold out for the lender's benefit. Our project was obviously targeted for the same treatment. I also found that the principal owners of the REIT had ties to the Mafia. One of my investors told me that when tempers heated up in a crucial meeting, the lender offered to, "Buy him a pair of concrete boots."

I also learned that one of the REIT's problem loans involved an abandoned gaudy motel in Daytona Beach, the *Roman Holiday* (each room had its own swimming pool and a female nude painted on the wall). I suggested that our company purchase this 'dog motel' by assuming the loan. to allow the REIT to take the bad loan off their books, in exchange for completion of the funding of the high-rise building. Since the lender REIT was under pressure from its investors -- because of the bad motel loan -- the concept was approved by them. I explained our strategy to them by telephone.

"If you fail to complete the funding for the *Villager* as agreed, we intend to impute the acquisition of the *Roman Holiday Motel* as usury interest and you will repay us double the loan to build the *Villager Condominium.*"

We had our attorneys prepare the documents for the purchase of the "dog motel" in such a way that, if necessary, we could impute the cost of the motel purchase to our loan to construct the *Villager.* This would make the loan usurious (over 18%) and the REIT would be in violation of Florida Law. The lenders' attorneys were aware of our intent and twice amended the documents to thwart our defense. Our investors notified the lender that the proposed changes were *unacceptable.* The REIT finally decided to approve the original documents.

Payments again flowed, but the final 10 percent was withheld, even after final completion of the building. Our people brought an action in the Courts of Brevard County against the REIT, alleging usury. The hearing before Judge Strown lasted several hours.

Finally, His Honor said,

"I am going on vacation and plan to continue this case in 30 days. In the meantime," and he turned to look directly at the lender's co-owner, "I suggest you come to a settlement because, frankly, I don't know how I am going to rule."

In the resultant settlement, our investors' ownership was reaffirmed and all 80 units were subsequently sold at a profit. The *Roman Holiday Inn* was returned to the REIT. A year later, the co-owner of the REIT boarded an airplane on which I was travelling. He stopped by my seat and said,

"Gardner, borrowers always try to claim usury, but you were the only one to make it stick. We were impressed. We have a problem for which we need your help. Are you interested."

Yes, I guess not!

How to Keep a Good Guy Investor from Becoming a Bad Guy.

The time arrived for my Exit Plan to come true. The date to actually capitalize came about earlier than I had planned because of two *unacceptable* -- to me -- business realities. First, I slept fitfully because I was co-signed on a substantial bank loan in Oklahoma. I discovered that my conservative nature did not handle that kind of exposure well.

The thrust of my four associates' argument was to use owner capital, with heavy emphasis on (necessary) debt financing. We shared equal ownership in *Borinquen Towers,* a huge high-rise project, a development of 1,000 homes, the *San Patricio Shopping Center,* and two tax-exempt factories.

One associate was a successful developer, another an attorney skilled in real estate law. The third was the owner of a huge midwestern chain of supermarkets, and the fourth, a young builder-developer who basically "ran the show."

I could have lived with anxiety-disrupted sleep, because of a multimillion dollar carrot, but not with the second reality. Every few months the three U.S. based investors came to the island of Puerto Rico. They loved to relax by the *Caribe Hilton Hotel* pool, then visit the casino late each evening. Around midnight we adjourned to one of the suites and began to negotiate the structuring of the 'next deal'.

A sumptuous midnight dinner, via room service, was followed by more discussions. About 3:00 a.m. -- and never earlier -- the 5 of us investors gathered around the table to sign checks, pro-rata to 20 percent ownership each. It came to me forcefully that I did not enjoy this ritual. So, I implemented my exit.

"I just realized that you four enjoy this," I said during a lull in the conversation. I immediately had their attention. "I don't. So, I want out."

There was at least a full minute of silence, then one investor said,

"Gardner, if you can't afford to stay in, we will see you get your money back."

The Good Guy was about to become the Bad Guy investor! I replied,

"I can handle it fine, but I'd rather spend more time with my family. I talked with my attorney and asked him if he would buy my stock for $150,000 and he assured me he would be delighted."

I knew that the four shareholders regretted not including a "right of first refusal" clause in our orginal Agreement. In addition, they disliked that particular attorney. I waited for the impact of my statement to change their thinking. It was true -- I had a firm commitment from the attorney.

"But since we are friends, I will offer my shares of common stock to you for somewhat less than his offer."

The deal was made. We settled for $125,000 I was released from all bank and other obligations. And, like one of my early heroes, Rainsford -- the ultimate innovator in *The Most Dangerous Game* by Richard Connell -- said after his final life or death encounter, *"(he) had never slept in a better bed..."* I slept the night through without a care, and made a policy decision to never again personally guarantee any debt negotiating talk. My business life follows a different drummer because:

CHAPTER TWELVE []

YOU NEVER HAVE ANYTHING UNTIL YOU SELL SOMETHING

The False Promise of Net Worth.The Exhilaration of Redeeming "Sweat Equity." You Never Have Anything Until You Sell Something. How to Sell a Company. How to Get the Best Price. How to Begin Again. Building Resources for the Retreading Years

T**he False Promise of Net Worth**
High net worth and book value tend to obscure a reality, which is expressed by a definition I once heard of a millionaire builder:

> **Rule.** *A millionaire builder is one who leases a new convertible, drives around with the top down with a new young blonde wife and her poodle, redecorates his apartment, and can raise $25,000 if his banker pushes him to the wall.*

The Exhilaration of Redeeming "Sweat Equity"

There has been no greater 'high' in my business life than to realize, at a closing of the Sale and Purchase Agreement, the tangible financial rewards of equity appreciation and recapture of deferred compensation. Prior financial sacrifices are forgotten. Every dollar of deferred fees has multiplied for my benefit.

There is a magic in this process which permits a mini-investment -- plus a lot of hard work -- to return 200, 500, 1,000 percent or even more on the original investment. Obviously, those able to experience such a high ROI are the creator-innovators who keep their day jobs, or have outside income to meet living expenses.

In the profitable sale of stock of assets in various ventures, amounts paid to me for my ownership interests brought a warm, fuzzy feeling of achievement. However, that feeling was never the spontaneous mental fist pump of joy which came from closing on a sale of stock or assets, where unstinting *sweat equity* is rewarded. In such cases, it is as if something substantial has been created out of nearly nothing. Net worth does not necessarily equate to liquidity, nor does it contribute to *gelt* formation. Companies can and do choke for cash flow -- even fail -- even though their book value is substantial. Holding on too long may be detrimental to one's financial health.

You Never Have Anything Until You Sell Something

The reality of the above-described millionaire builder is sobering. And, as previously noted, there are entrepreneurs who invest everything they have in the first venture and incur a heavy load of debt. Total net profits after taxes are invested in new machinery, equipment, etc. As the enterprise grows, they and their families have little or nothing. Typically the home is heavily mortgaged. There is no gelt, no discretionary funds, and little or no flexibility. On paper, they may be multi-millionaires. But they are living proof of the saying,

"You never have anything until you sell something."

"But why sell the stock or assets of that first venture if it is profitable and shows every evidence that it will continue to be successful?"

That is a good question. My response is:

1. If the owner has a specific Exit Plan to sell that first venture upon reaching a certain net worth, or profitability, or other measurement (unless there is an obvious windfall or bonanza), he or she should not be tempted to continue ownership in the company beyond that prescribed in the Exit Plan.

2. A profitable business should be able to command a purchase price of five to eight times the average annual NPBT of the previous 3 years (a simple multiplier-type business valuation formula, which varies according to total book value and fixed assets). A small company with average earnings of $100,000 annually can--all other things being equal-- capitalize for $500.000, a good enabling sum.

3. Most new enterprises have a specific life-span. The fact that 5 years is spoken of as the 'half-life' of a business is truer than some would like to acknowledge. And companies that continue to be successful after 10 years are in the minority. Our filter factory is an exception -- no better product has yet been designed for the drip irrigation market.

4. Entrepreneurs tend to live in a state of anxiety until they 'sell something.' It is remarkable how much more sanguine they become after exiting the business with large amounts of capital in hand. With it, the entrepreneur can satisfy nearly *all* his or her needs; create or purchase a new venture; set aside rainy day funds (gelt); provide a comfortable living

and security for the family; and enjoy steady income from invested capital in preparation for the *retreading years*.

How to Sell a Company

. The Company with A Full Management Team.

A management team is a prerequisite to attract venture capital firms, which, if the owner is not averse to giving up 30 percent ownership or more, can help the company achieve second and third stage growth.

Likewise, many potential Buyers--individuals and companies-- before considering an acquisition, require that an in-depth management team be in place. Using the example of a typical manufacturing operation, such an organization might include a President/CEO, Financial Vice President, Marketing Vice President, General Manager, Plant Manager, etc.

The transfer of ownership scarcely causes a blip in the progress of the business, because the stand-alone team will continue to operate without interruption under the new owners. This is the type of company which is most readily saleable because it requires no additional management.

The Company Without a Management Team.

Many enterprises are basically sole proprietorships where the owner(s) manages the company, with one or two low-to-middle-level employees. At most, there may be a General Manager and/or Sales Manager who work under the direction of the owner. Assuming that the owner wishes to capitalize and leave the company, the market for potential Buyers will, for the most part, be limited to several sources:

1. Those who have available, and can contribute, management resources to replace the former working

owner of the company.

2. Competitors, who already have management in place, see this type of company as an ideal acquisition. They already have a management team, and the acquisition will allow general and administrative burden to be spread across a greater volume of total sales. A side benefit is an upward nudge in profits as price pressure is reduced.

3. Individual manager-investors who look to 'step into the shoes' of the exiting owner by acquiring the business and providing the necessary resources and management to take the business to the next stage.

In an entrepreneur's various ventures during his or her business life cycle, all of the Exit Plans noted above may be used -- and more. My *exits* to date have been as follows:

- The common voting stock of the plastics manufacturing company was sold to a competitor, who had management available.
- Assets of the filter business were purchased by the leading competitor, with management available.
- Common voting shares of stock in multiple manufacturing, housing and commercial development ventures were acquired by my associates.
- The electronics factory shares of common voting stock were transferred in an *involuntary* sale to co-owners. in an exciting triumph over an intended for "10 cents on a dollar."
- A Fiber Broom factory which was sold to the principal vendor.

How to Get the Best Price.

In the past few years, there has been an explosion in the number of companies providing business valuations. Part of this sudden growth is due to more frequent requests by the IRS for independent, third-party appraisals of decedents' estates.

Certified Public Accountants have discovered business valuation as a valuable adjunct to their business. Many CPA firms which offer this service have a Certified Valuation Analyst (CVA) on their staff.

To obtain the title of CVA, a candidate must complete a course of study offered by the *National Association of Certified Valuation Analysts* (for current lists of CVAs in each state, contact them at 1245 East Brickyard Road, Salt Lake City, Utah, or via the Internet at *http://www.nacva. com/index.htm.).*

Depending on complexity, business valuation of a small business might require 20 to 40 hours of the CVA's time, at rates that vary from $150 to $350 per hour. By applying different formulas and approaches, a CVA is often able to improve the net return to the Seller.

A few years ago, there were only two or three business valuation specialists in all of Florida. I, personally, studied all the applicable formulas and applied them to reach the highest justifiable selling price for our factory. Then I enlisted the services of a business valuation specialist to confirm my analysis. The third-party recommendation provided leverage to ultimately establish a higher selling price for the company's assets. Almost always, additional amounts can be obtained by non-compete agreements. etc.

In most cases, when the time comes to implement the exit plan, it is advantageous toward the successful sale of a company or its assets to have a recent business valuation at hand. It adds credibility and a climate of confidence, as do annual financial reports prepared by one of the major public accounting firms.

When there is evidence of serious interest in acquiring the company, it is vital to pre-qualify the potential Buyer. Ask about previous investments. Get banking and business references. Contact all possible sources. Order a personal credit check. There are many Internet credit services. My attorney recently 'pulled' a *fast-track* credit report mainly for probate purposes, which was startling in its detail.

After doing the above due diligence, the Seller should be able to determine the following:

(a) Is the Buyer able and willing to perform? (Some are able, but unwilling, and vice versa.)

(b) Does the Buyer have a history of *milking* an acquired company and letting it go back to the Seller. (It can be so unrewarding to receive a down payment, then find out it is the *only* payment one will ever receive, and then have to pick up the pieces of the company.)

(c) Will the Buyer provide sufficient references and information for the Seller to make an informed judgment? If not, tell the Buyer that the only acceptable offer is "C.I.F". Should he or she ask what that means, smile and say, "Cash-in-Fist."

When negotiations begin, the Buyer may inquire as to the 'asking price'. Never divulge the desired price at this stage. A good answer might be:

"That depends on the terms. One amount would be acceptable as a cash offer, another for short-term, and still another for long-term. Which do you have in mind?"

This avoids a direct answer to the question, while suggesting that the owner might accept extended terms of payment if necessary, to obtain a higher selling price.

At the appropriate moment in the negotiations, bring out the most optimistic CVA business valuation, 'just as a point of reference.' Convince the Buyer to make an initial offer. If it is 'in the ball park,' agree to it in principle, then negotiate it upward. Use that wonderful word *'unacceptable'* when necessary to establish 'go-no-go' parameters in the negotiations (this term comes from 'go-no-go' gauges which precisely measure critical openings, such as the gap in a spark plug or distributor points on an automobile).

When the best offer is on the table and there is basic agreement on the total purchase price, there are ways, through the use of 'add-ons,' to increase the selling price by *as much as 10 percent.*

Example: "Are you interested in a non-compete agreement? (Most buyers are.) Do you prefer to include a non-compete clause in the Purchase Agreement, or in a separate side-letter agreement? Would a 5-year non-compete agreement be acceptable?"

Start with an amount of compensation (equal to 5 percent of the total selling price); as consideration not to compete with the company. Approval will usually be forthcoming. Then present the second add-on.

"We are still a little apart on the purchase price..." (pause) "As you know, I have a long-term loan with the company. Rather than deduct it from the selling price, would you be willing to carry it on the books until we work out a mutually acceptable way to handle it?"

The loan, which the owner should have had on the books for at least a year prior to the sale, and been paying interest at an rate acceptable to IRS, could be an amount equal to approximately 5 to 10 percent of the desired selling price.

The Buyer agrees, in a side letter, to write the loan off after a period of time. At that time the Seller will be obligated to pay capital gains tax on the imputed income.

How to Begin Again

The entrepreneur who quits his or her day job. and sells substantial stock or assets to family and friends, and in effect sacrifices all available resources upon the altar of The First Venture, truly 'goes for broke'. Unfortunately, should the first attempt fail, there could be *nothing left with which to begin again*. It might require 3, 5, or more years to pay off debt secured with personal signatures, pacify relatives and friends who suffered losses, generate a modicum of seed capital, and then organize a second enterprise.

> **Rule.** *One signature can and will place the signer behind the 'power curve' and dictate the course of his or her life for years.*

As an Advisor to several Boards of Directors and Boards of Trustees, I was asked to meet with each Division Manager, to review personal, business and financial situations and goals. One person had committed everything to a previous venture, as noted above. Though the manufactured product showed good innovation and creativity, the company foundered. The ongoing debt service taxed his salaried income.

He considered filing for protection under federal bankruptcy laws, but agreed to a plan to work with creditors, which brought greater proficiency to his work and generated more personal income. Today he is free of back debt and is rebuilding his asset base. But nearly 4 years have elapsed in the process.

It is preferable to hold in reserve enough capital for a

'second try,' in the event of a first failure.

I vividly remember how Dorothy, my accountant, showed me that even in the most dire financial situation, cash can be set aside. In the first stage of our initial venture, when meeting each weekly payroll was a real challenge, she told me that with our new baby, she needed a second automobile.

"Honey, you know our cash flow better than I. We just can't afford a second car."

She didn't say anything, so I felt the matter had been successfully set aside. Not long thereafter, she announced she had a new (used) car.

"You see, I've been expensing $50 every week for quite awhile," she announced.

I was momentarily speechless. But that is how I learned that one can expense a small weekly amount in any business for a specific need -- without causing harm to the business.

Whether the new enterprise is a start-up or acquired from a third party, it is important that a limit be set on the entrepreneur's total investment. My own policy has been to invest up to $20,000 in stock and/or loans in each venture (no increase allowed for inflation over 3 decades) with no personal signatures from myself or my wife, but with all necessary sweat equity.

Like most entrepreneurs, I do not knowingly take risks. After achieving our gelt and discretionary funds, it seemed almost unseemly never to have taken a risk, never to have reached for the gold ring.

A suitable opportunity arose in a revolutionary (but unsuccessful) technique to recover micron gold in the four corners area (Utah. Colorado, Nevada. Arizona. and New Mexico). We invested $40,000 (which we designated as "throw-at-the-wall-money-to-see-what sticks" in a secondary recovery placer mine in the Four Corners area in Utah, along the Dolores River. The gold is still there.

> **Rule**. *Since there is no guarantee that the new enterprise will succeed, commit only a portion of available assets, in order to launch a second venture if necessary. A successful business is often the product of one or more previous failures.*

Building Resources for the Retreading Years

Retirement programs, pensions, 401k plans, ESOPs, etc. are usually not part of the entrepreneur's lexicon. For several reasons, the entrepreneur's business activity falls outside these 'safety nets'. True, Social Security benefits are basically at the same level as the lifetime employees, but funds only one-third to one-half of the cost of living of a retiree, and promises to be less in the future.

Most retirement plans are based on measurements of time/value such as a certain number of years of continuous employment, employee contributions to pension plans, vesting, insurance policies, etc. The creator-innovator, without the option of traditional retirement plans, has no choice but to provide a comprehensive self-retirement plan toward a comfortable retirement, and to avoid *retreading* (the necessity of continuing to work) when retirement money is no longer sufficient.

Since there is rarely a retirement plan in place from the various ventures, (cash flow needs of the business always seem to pre-empt such niceties as retirement plans) *gelt* must be set aside so that interest on the invested capital will defray ongoing living expenses. Today, if personal retirement income of $50,000 a year is required, at least $1,000,000 must be working to produce this amount..

We pass along to the reader a simple financial plan which works for us. It calls for approximately one-third of total assets to be in income-producing residential revenue from single or duplex housing (with a goal to become mortgage-free by retirement age); another third in U.S. Treasury bills which can be purchased direct from a Federal Reserve Bank, and/or Time Deposits in the form of FDIC secured instruments (Certificates of Deposit now insured up to $250,000); and the remaining third in investments which we control. We have also opted to self-insure, except for modest insurance policies purchased years ago. If the reader notes the absence of stock market investments in the above, I can make no comment, since we have never had the talent to prosper in that arena.

> **Rule**. *By staying with a conservative, reduced-risk investment plan, the entrepreneur will inevitably be judged either unenlightened or brilliant, based solely on changes in economic conditions.*

Example: Years ago the real estate market was booming. The Manager of our local Citibank chided us for not investing in Florida real estate, and the stock market, and for being too conservative. He shook his head, and informed us the world and our business friends were passing us by.

Then came a severe recession. A close friend, faced with the complaints of his wife when he announced he could no longer afford the annual trip of three months to Spain, turned and ran off their luxurious penthouse patio into space. Another friend suffered a heart attack when unable to make payments on mortgages on his Florida real estate.

The same bank manager congratulated us for being so astute, noting that "cash was king," and I was one of the few able to benefit. He urged me to follow his example and liquidate all our assets. I thanked him and we kept doing what we had been -- and still are -- doing. It works.

CHAPTER THIRTEEN ⏸

A FEW KEY OBSERVATIONS
Starting that New Venture - Basic Requirements - Location for the New Business -Applicable Tax Law and City, County, State and Other Federal Laws and Regulations - Evolution of Regulatory Pollution - Profit-and-Loss and Cash Flow Projections- "That Three Percent Purely Adds Up"-Presentation and Communications Skills - Ability To Envision Alternate Products or Services - The Key is to Maximize Resources.

Starting that New Venture

Characteristics of an entrepreneurial venture are: (1) a need is identified, (2) a product or service market niche is evaluated and validated, and (3) *added value* is created in a new or existing enterprise. Starting a business where new value is added is almost always entrepreneurial. Acquiring a retail bus
iness with an existing customer base where it is difficult to add value (travel agency, automotive repair shop, quick-copy store, flower shop, etc.) may or not meet the criteria for entrepreneurship. It is rarely possible to create new markets or devise new products or service applications in such entities. Little new value is created. Sales may increase due to new management style and personality or better use of resources and more creative advertising, but the basic business entity remains the same.

HOW TO MAKE BAD GUYS FINISH LAST

Basic Requirements

Those starting a new business need to know certain basic requirements including:

a. Location for the new business.
b. Applicable tax law and city, county, state, and other federal laws and regulations.
c. Business tools: profit-and-loss, cash flow projections and business plans.
d. Computer literacy as to word processing and spread-sheets.
e. Presentation and communication skills.
f. Ability to envision alternate products or services.
g. Ability to turn adverse situations to advantage.
h. Nearly every business is inadequately financed; the key is to maximize available resources.
i. A product or service must be timely and viable as determined by the available market.

Location for the New Business

A basic rule of real estate is that the three most important requirements for a project are: "Location. Location. Location." This is applicable to start-up enterprises as well. There are two common errors in business site selection. The first is the human tendency to select a location on a 'gut feeling', on the basis of impulse rather than due diligence.

There is something about the sight of a vacant storefront in an otherwise fully-leased shopping center that triggers feelings of optimism and need for ownership. But it rarely pays to try to adopt a specific space to a business. The needs of the business should govern the selection of suitable space.

Example: During the past decade, three attempts have been made to open an ice cream store in a small strip shopping center near my home. Ignoring reality, the last owner, like the previous two, "just knew" it would be a prime location for an ice cream shop. Yet, even the most modest market survey would have indicated there is no real market niche. Within a year he joined the lament of his predecessors: *"To heck with the cheese. Let me out of the trap!"*

Within a radius of 5 miles, two similar businesses flourish. There is no apparent reason why consumers of frozen treats prefer to drive to these less attractive places of no better quality or price. They just do. A fourth candidate will probably come forward to reopen that ice cream shop. This is the *law of the next optimist* and the lifeblood of the business broker.

The second most common error is to select an overly expensive location and appoint it with costly furniture and fixtures to acquire a perceived status and dignity for the new enterprise when it is not really indicated. There is no need, for example, to locate a drop-ship wholesale catalog sporting goods business (where the manufacturer ships direct to the customer) in an expensive office building. Because, by the very nature of catalog sales, buyers rarely visit the place of business. The owner goes to the customers. A small office and a post office box would be sufficient.

The true entrepreneur rarely feels the need for ostentation or even creature comfort. Many owners of small manufacturing companies continue to work out of cramped, Spartan offices, in spite of the fact that their business is flourishing. Of course, if the start-up business depends on walk-in or drive-in trade, the space must be in a well-visited location and be attractive and inviting.

A rule-of-thumb is to lease the lowest cost space suitable for first and perhaps second year operations. Storage mini-warehouses or business incubators are often a good initial solution.

As the business grows, expandable flex-space, such as a warehouse and/or manufacturing area with adjunct offices, may be warranted. As the venture expands, the decision whether to lease, build or buy property becomes important. If working capital is tied up in the too-early acquisition of a building, it could be a fatal blow to the business.

It might, however, be advantageous to build or buy a building if a modest down payment can be made from discretionary funds and monthly mortgage payments are the same or slightly more than equivalent rent or lease payments. Assuming the selection of owned space is in a good location, there is an opportunity for property to appreciate.

Applicable Tax Law and City, County, State and Other Federal Laws and Regulations

If a location looks too good to be true, it probably is. It is vital to ascertain in advance if proposed operations are possible at the proposed site. Zoning and deed restrictions may limit the use. And there may be an insurmountable burden of regulatory caveats as federal, state, county and city agencies -- which habitually swell upon their granted authority -- become *Bad Guys*.

The Food and Drug Administration (FDA) can be a real bogeyman. Even if a new product has a verified market niche, if it is found to be subject to FDA approval, one might be advised to develop an alternate product to avoid the extreme costs and delays of obtaining said approvals. It is not uncommon for companies to spend tens of thousands of dollars and devote many months, often years, to this process.

Also ready to be Bad Guys are various Water Authorities ("Sorry, your property has just been reclassified to wetlands"), the U.S. Army Corps of Engineers ("The impact study will *only* take 6 months to a year"), and the Environmental Protection Agency ("There are buried tanks of solvents under your building lot. You can't build until it's cleaned up.")

In addition, there are OSHA, city and county commissions, building and fire departments and others, all with veto power over the start-up.

There are many horror stories of companies installed at considerable cost which never begin operating because such agencies aggressively apply their interpretation of rules and regulations. It is interesting, but not surprising, that while these government agencies were originally created for the greater good of the community (and indeed have done much to promote clean water and healthy, uncontaminated earth and atmosphere), they have often pushed the outer limits of their original empowerment. It's when these agencies swell on their authority and stifle new businesses that they must be considered *Bad Guys*.

In our over-regulated communities, these *business contaminants* seem to be everywhere. Typically staffed with consummate bureaucrats who enjoy nearly unlimited power, they frequently exhibit a jaundiced attitude, tinged with jealousy, toward the world of business. An unknown author once described public employees' view of business as follows:

> *"They are like so many gray-green*
> *trolls under a gray-green bridge, fighting*
> *over the last moldy gray-green piece of*
> *hæese."*

Laws and regulations designed to protect endangered animals, birds, and plants tend to stifle creation of new businesses if over-zealously applied. In central Florida, for instance, an endangered scrub jay subspecies, if observed flitting across your property, is enough to halt development. Thus, owners of vacant land tend to keep their land denuded to discourage the little bird from visiting. Well-meaning authorities have cleared land of stands of trees to provide scrub jay habitat, and are embarrassed that the jay does not move in. At the same time, they have removed picnic tables to discourage scrub jay visitors in at least one local park because scrub jays came to indulge their passion for peanuts.

Several years ago another tiny bird, a species of flicker, caused millions of dollars of damage and delay by pecking over 100 holes in the insulation of the Space Shuttle as it stood ready for launch. NASA officials were paralyzed at first by a 'fear-to-offend' local environmentalists, but finally took steps to discourage the birds' enthusiastic drilling.

Evolution of Regulatory Pollution

It is my personal belief -- garnered from the study of history and decades of firsthand observation -- that our burgeoning regulatory *pollution* is not due so much to bad intent as to the inevitable result of elapsed time. For more than 200 years of our great nation's existence, our legislative, quasi-legislative and administrative bodies have striven to create new laws, rules and regulations to respond to changing conditions. Indeed, their creators' stature (at least in Congress) is measured in large part by the number of bills successfully sponsored and voted into law. Ever-increasing restrictive and regulatory impediments are a natural by-product of our country's aging process. This is not surprising, as it is a known fact that bureaucratic overburden pollutes all older societies.

Example: In one Latin American nation, after being notified that an unspecified gift awaited me at the *Aduana,* (Customs), I spent the day buying official stamps, walking a set of documents back and forth to be signed, initialled and stamped, completing *trámites (TRAW-me-tays)* -- a wonderful Spanish word with no one-word English equivalent that means bureaucratic 'make-work' requirements.

After completing 12 trámites in as many different offices, an exorbitant duty was assessed. I insisted on seeing my gift before paying the duty. It turned out to be a stale box of chocolates from a well-meaning friend in the United States. I bowed and handed the battered package to the stony-faced custom's officer,

> *"Que lo disfrute!"* ("Enjoy!")

It is rare for an older country to strip off regulatory overburden accumulated over centuries and return to its entrepreneurial origins. New nations rarely invent regulatory burden because of their need to create infrastructure and gross national product. The good news is that with all our regulatory woes, we have not (yet) reached the level of bureaucratic burden common to many other nations in Europe and Latin America.

Profit-and-Loss and Cash Flow Projections

One of the most important business tools for the new enterprise is the business plan, with accompanying profit-and-loss and cash flow projections. Many owners and managers of new businesses shy away from (or are too impatient with) the business plan concept. Ignorant of the elements and benefits of such a plan, and/or untrained in its use, they often do not know either their 'markups' or costs. One exception is illustrated in an anecdote, supposedly true.

HOW TO MAKE BAD GUYS FINISH LAST

That *Three Percent Purely Adds Up*

"Billy-Bob, you have a profitable junk business. How do you do it, when you can neither read nor write?"

"Well, Ah buys for $1.00 and Ah sells for $4.00, and that *3 percent purely adds up.*"

With such a "3 percent" (actually 300 percent) markup this business needs no business plan. But most do. There are easily understood, straightforward books in nearly every library which detail how to create business plans, profit-and-loss statements and cash flow projections. For the computer literate, inexpensive software programs are available which follow a step-by-step format, but they may suffer from an overkill of detail.

Projections for 1, 2, 3, and even 5 years can be laboriously prepared by hand with a calculator, as they nearly all were until a decade ago, prior to the widespread use of the personal computer. Large green-lined pads are still available providing for 15 or more columns (for months, subtotals and totals), and up to 100 rows (for sales, direct costs, indirect costs, fixed and variable sales, administrative expenses, etc.).

However, a model projection prepared by hand is cumbersome and cannot easily be used for 'what-if' scenarios. In contrast, a computer spreadsheet will, after all direct and indirect costs and fixed and variable expenses are entered -- using a recurring formula -- instantly display both the projected Net Profit Before Taxes (NPBT) and the cash flow needs monthly and annually. So, *what if* sales might be lower and costs higher? No problem. The new figures are keyed in, columns and rows change instantly, and revised profits (or losses) along with cash requirements, are forecast almost immediately.

HOW TO BECOME A SUCCESSFUL ENTREPRENEUR

It is important in the start-up phase of a new enterprise that the entrepreneur learn -- if at all possible -- at least minimal keyboard (typing) skills and become computer literate in spreadsheets and word processing. Personal computers (IBM-compatible or Apple Macintosh) and printers are affordable for any business owner, and often come with word processing and spreadsheet programs already installed. Almost any generic spreadsheet software program will suffice for projection purposes. Most have evolved from the formulas of Visicalc. Software programs for word processing, invoice preparation, mailings, check writing, mail-merge, etc. are inexpensive, ubiquitous and mostly user friendly.

An early spreadsheet program for personal computers was *Visicalc*. Prior to the advent of the first IBM PC® in the early 1980's, this program was typically operated on a Model II, Tandy (Radio Shack)® personal computer at a hardware/software cost of from $7,500 to $8,500. Although ingenious, Visicalc had an unfriendly user's guide. To learn *replicate* and *ranges* concepts (i.e., to cause subsequent columns and rows on the spreadsheet to automatically compute from a formula applied to the first column and row) required a true gift of discernment. One could have wished for a Biblical *Urim and Thummin* in order to translate it.

Should the entrepreneur not feel comfortable with business plan preparation and the supporting profit-and-loss and cash flow projections, there are financial and business consultants who will, for a fee, provide these basic business tools and update them as needed. Accountants or CPAs are reluctant to generate such reports because it is not cost effective for them, and is alien to their main professional activity, which is reporting the past, not forecasting the future.

The entrepreneur should not only become familiar with computers but, where possible, learn to perform *all* the operations of the budding enterprise. Today there are many viable, easy-to-use spreadsheet programs.

Ability to perform financial, administrative, marketing, sales, production and clerical tasks will help make the entrepreneur self-reliant. Then, as the business grows, the owner is never completely dependent on any employee. It is beneficial for each employee to be aware that the owner-manager can do his or her job in an emergency.

Example: For many years, one of my tests of a new secretary or administrative assistant, as they are now usually designated, was to dictate a letter. If the letter came back to me for signature with errors and/or carelessly corrected 'strikeovers.' I turned to my typewriter or computer, produced the letter error free, signed and placed it in the out-basket. A few minutes later the employee was back in my office.

"This is not the letter I typed."

"That's right,"

I would respond quietly with a disarming smile. From that moment, every letter placed on my desk for signature was error free, or carefully corrected.

Presentation and Communications Skills

Of the hundreds of entrepreneurs I have known, most were able -- in one way or another -- to communicate the basic concepts required to market their new or improved product or services and to obtain needed resources. For instance, it is relatively easy to obtain credit from vendors. They are basically optimistic and usually only seek modest assurance of payment for materials or services. And, if the product or service fills a specific need, customers do not require a great communicator. Likewise, bankers are less interested in the communication skills of the owner of a venture than they are in assets and ability to repay the loan. Thus, it's not surprising to find that -- except for the most eccentric, introverted and withdrawn individuals -- an entrepreneur's dedication, willingness to learn, enthusiasm and belief in a niche-filling product or service will usually suffice to obtain needed resources and customers.

Being able to communicate ideas and make good presentations, however, is of great importance to the ultimate success of an enterprise. To achieve or refine this attribute, the entrepreneur will need to practice. Like Demosthenes, one of history's great orators, who overcame a speech impediment by speaking for countless hours to an imaginary audience with his mouth full of pebbles, the entrepreneur can learn more effective communication by trial, error and practice.

Ability to Envision Alternate Products or Services

Entrepreneurs must have the creative ability to develop alternate products or services and additional markets in the event the initial venture's niche does not materialize as planned.

Example: A number of years ago, three of us investors organized a company to manufacture acrylic (plexiglass) gift items such as breakfast trays, gift boxes, novelties, etc. One shareholder supplied raw materials from his plastics scrap company, mainly low-cost acrylic offcuts. My small investment company provided financing and general management. The third shareholder was a skilled plastics technician/plant manager.

Production began, but the market failed to develop. It was necessary to either close the business or develop new markets. As an emergency measure to provide positive cash flow, we purchased two sets of wood molds at a bargain price for three-dimensional 12- and 24-inch vacuum-formed plastic letters, and began an intensive local marketing effort. Soon, nearly all the companies in the area displayed their names on the front wall of their buildings, in three-dimensional acrylic vacuum-molded letters in bright colors.

With the resultant cash infusion we created a new product, then discontinued the manufacture of discretionary consumer products. We designed patterns and manufactured molds for products needed in the housing industry: clear acrylic sky domes, vacuum-formed plastic bi-fold closet doors, vanities, and a series of indoor and outdoor lights. The business became successful and the shareholders benefited from the income tax-exempt sale of the firm, 5 years later, to a public company.

Again, several years ago I provided management consulting services to a group of real estate investors. One of their projects was a motel at an intersection with I-95 in Central Florida. The other three corners of the intersection were vacant land. The motel project had been authenticated by a feasibility study prepared by a leading motel consulting firm. We were surprised to note, a month or so later, that land was being cleared to build another motel in the northeast quadrant. Within the year a third motel was constructed on the southwest corner. The market was overbuilt.

How did this happen? Three motel consulting firms independently developed favorable feasibility studies for one motel each at the intersection. All three consultants later claimed that they had no knowledge of the other studies. The result? The tourist market was woefully inadequate to support the hundreds of rooms built. The owners of one motel sought protection under federal bankruptcy laws. Another was subsidized in various changes of ownership, until natural market growth and tourism increased occupancy rates to profitability.

There were few alternate uses for a low-occupancy motel. My clients, owners of the initial motel, enhanced their cash flow by converting units to cottage industries and offices until, finally, the growing tourist market brought profitability to all three motels. This was the best solution available at the time. Today there are companies which specialize in converting such properties to attractive mini-storage warehouse spaces financed by pension funds. A prime example is the *Fontainbleu* motel in New Orleans. Processed through the RTC, it has been converted to an upscale mini-warehouse complex.

Many enterprises may, at any given time, defy the creation of alternate products and/or services to supplant the originally-designated market when it caps out or fails to materialize. But the innovative entrepreneur will find ways to increase cash flow if there is any alternate market niche at all, and be poised for future market innovations.

The Key is to Maximize Resources

It is true that there are successful entrepreneurs who have started their enterprises with "$50 or $100." But most ventures require substantial amounts of start-up and ongoing working capital or credit. If the entrepreneur has savings, but little or no other income, it is impressive how fast the nest egg disappears in daily living expenses. And should two entrepreneurs join in an enterprise and both require living wages, their combined savings vanish exponentially. Outside investors or lenders are understandably reluctant to provide capital to subsidize the entrepreneur's living costs. And there is always inertia in obtaining third party start-up funding for the enterprise, due to the high mortality rate of new businesses.

HOW TO MAKE BAD GUYS FINISH LAST

One solution for the owner is to keep his or her 'day job' and not look to Newco for expenses or salary while providing the effort necessary to make it a success. There are advantages to this approach. By providing 'sweat equity' initial sales translate into higher profits, which   if scrupulously reinvested in inventory, tooling, machinery and equipment, will result in lower production costs and increased profits, maximizing financial resource

CHAPTER FOURTEEN ⟦

FIRST YOU LEARN - THEN YOU EARN - THEN YOU RETURN - (USING OPM)
The Author's Contribution

A few years ago I was talking wiith a friend of mine in the *Business School of Brigham Young University,* Idaho. In the couse of the coversation, he asked me to read a letter adressed to him, a year or so earlier, from the Dean of the *Marriott School for Entrepreneural Studies, Brigham Young Universuty, Provo, Utah,* which stated to the effect that:

"When *Brigham Young University Idaho* reaches donations of $50,000. the *Marriott School for Entrepreneurial Studies* will provide matching funds, to strengthen their efforts to develop *Entrepreneurial Studies.*"

I read the letter carefully. I said that I would get back to him in a few days. I called a good friend, who owed me a favor, and explained the situation. He called me back in a few days to indicate that a Foundation had accepted the proposal and would donate $50,000.

A few months later I was invited to attend *Brigam Young University Idaho* and participate in a panel discussion open to the student body, The two other participants were members of the *Founders Forum of Brigham Young University,*

Provo. Utah. As the students, 800 of them, filed in to take their seats, we engaged in casual conversation,

"We had to work hard to match the $50,000. We did not expect *Brigam Young University Idaho* to get their funds so quickly!" the man from the East remarked. Then he turned to me and made a point of looking me fixedly,

"And what brings you here?"

I smiled and replied,

"I am the reason you had to work so hard to match the $50,000 gift I obtained!"

The weeks went by. Then the thought came to me,

"Perhaps *Brigham Young University Hawaii* was sent the same letter from the *Marriott School for Entrepreneurial Studies.*"

I telephoned the Dean of the *Business School* at *Brigam Young University Hawaii* and he confirmed receipt of the same letter, promising matching funds of $50,000. should *Brigam Young University Hawaii* obtain donations in that same amount,

I called my client who had offered to 'do something special' for me that year, explained the reason for the requested donation, and asked,

"Dave, would you make a $10,000 donation in my name to *Brigam Young University Hawaii*?"

He agreed. I then telephoned a friend whom I knew loved Hawaii.

"Bob, I have $10,000," and explained the reason for my call. "Do you still have a love affair with Hawaii?"

He said he did.

"Could you come up with the other $40,000?"

Without hesitation, he achnowleged in the affirmative.

The new Dean at the Business School of *Brigam Young University Hawaii* was pleased to have $100,000. to stregthen their program to train entrepreneurs.

The Entrepreneurial program there was bolstered by a $2,500,000 gift in 2007.

In 2000, my client donated $30,000 in my name to create the *Gardner and Dorothy Russell Entrepreneurial Scholership Fund (*an Endowment) at *Brigham Young University Hawaii, Brigham Young University Idaho* and *Southern Virginia University,* at Buena Vista, Virginia.

At about the same time, I donated 300 copies of my book *The Effective Entrepreneur* to each of the four previously named Universities to be sold to sudents for $10.00 (Retail price was $14.99) - all proceeds to be utilized by the *Business School*. During my visits to *Brigham Young University Idaho, Brigham Young University Hawaii,* and *Southern Virginia University*, I was invited to teach a Chapter from my book and gloried in the experience. At one University I received a standing ovation from the students. My father, the ultimate in academe must have looked down with delight, and I was pleased.

When all 3000 copies of *The Effective Emtrepreneur* were shipped, with not even one book signing session, I received a letter from the Dean of the Business School of *Brigham Young University Idaho* requesting another 100 books. I decided not to reprint and called the Dean of the Marriott School at *Brigam Young University* Provo, Utah, secure in the knowledge that they had not utilized the book. and that they must have, in some dusty corner, copies that I could use for *Brigham Young University Hawaii*

The *Dean of the Marriott Scholl of Entrepneurial Studies of Brigham Young University, Provo* exclaimed:

HOW TO MAKE BAD GUYS FINISH LAST

"Gardner. the only copy of your book remaining at BYU is my personal copy. red-lined. and on the shelf in my office!"

HOW TO BECOME A SUCCESSFUL ENTREPRENEUR
<u>BIBLIOGRAPHY</u>

William Alarid	*Money Sources for Small Business* • Puma, 1991.
Rosabeth N. Canter	*The Change Masters* • Simon & Schuster, 1983.
Charles Coonradt	*The Game of Work* (Third Edition)
Clifford M. Baumbach & Joseph R. Mancuso	*Entrepreneurship&V entureM anagemente-Second Edition* • Prentice-Hall, 1987.
David H. Bangs, Jr.	*The Start Up Guide, A One-Year Plan for Entrepreneur*s • Upstart Publishing, Dover, NH, 1989.
Robert Benfari, PhD	*Understanding Your Management Style* • Lexington Books, 1991. (A thorough analysis of personality measurement beyond)
James C. Comiskey	*How to Start, Expand and Sell a Business* • Venture Perspectives Press, San Jose, CA 5th Printing 1989. (An excellent "How-To" publication.)
Peter F. Drucker	*Innovation and Entrepreneurship -- Practice and Principles* • Harper & Row, 1985. (Deep insight from the Master. The emphasis is on Internal Corporate Entrepreneurs.)
George Gilder	*Recapturing The Spirit of Enterprise -- Updated for the 1990s* • ICS Press, Institut for Contemporary Studies, San Francisco, CA, 1992.
Charles J. Givens	*Wealth Without Risk* • Simon & Schuster, 1988. (Valuable information for the entrepreneur.)
Arthur S. Grove Fred Klein	*High Output Management* • RandomHouse, *Handbook on Building a Profitable Business* • Entrepreneurial Workshops Publications, Seattle 1990. (120 questions. Good insight.)
Joseph R. Mancuso	*How to Start, Finance and Manage Your Own Business* • Prentice-Hall, 1978.

HOW TO MAKE BAD GUYS FINISH LAST

	Fun & Guts • Addison-Wesley Publishing Company, 1973.(Note This os one of more than 24 book by Mancuso. The Center for Entrepreneurial Management, Inc. 83 Spring Street,,New York City, NY 10012)
Judith H. McQuown	*Use Your Own Corporation to Get Rich* • Pocket Books, 1991.
Ted Nicholas	*Secrets of Entrepreneurial Leadership* Dearborn Publishing, Inc., 1993. (Refreshing thoughts on entrepreneurial management methods -- with forms.)
Geoffrey N. Smith &Paul Brown	*Sweat Equity* • Simon & Schuster,
Linda Pinson	*The Home-Based Entrepreneur* • Out of Your Mind and into the Marketplace,
David Robinson	*What Is An Entrepreneur?* • Bob Adams, Inc. Publishers, 1990.
Jeffry A. Timmons	*The Entrepreneurial Mind* • Brick House Publishing Company, 1989. (Important thoughts -- see Chapter 8, "What Skills Are Needed for Excellent Self-Evaluation. Also Chapter 12.)
Karl H. Vesper	*Frontiers of Entrepreneurship Research* • Babson College.

———

Internet Sources   http://www.thinkinglike.com/Entrepreneur-Word/Entrepreneur-Book-titles.htm

APPENDIX

Chapter I - *Understanding Your Management Style*
(The following has merit, but needs to be reviewed
and evaluated. I don't understand all of it.)
Additional Measurements for Management Style:
The MBTI, by Katherine and Isobel Briggs

Karl Jung's theory of classic Psychological Types is the
background for the MBTI tests for personality definition,
developed by Katherine Briggs and her daughter, Isobel,
after World War II. According to Jung, everybody is either
Extrovert (E) or Introvert (I), and there are two rational or
judgment functions, thinking (T) and feeling (F), and two
irrational or perception functions, sensing (S) and intuition
(N). There are four possible combinations of the four functions: sensation and thinking (ST); sensation and feeling
(SF); intuition and thinking (NT); and intuition and feeling
(NT).

The extroverted types are: EST, ESF, ENT, ENF. The
introverted types are: IST, ISF, INT, INF. Thus, there are
8 types. The essence of the MBTI is that the Briggs have
identified 8 additional personality measurements types, for
a total of 16. They added Perceiving (P) and Judging (J) to
describe the person who uses either sensing or intuition in
these interactions (P), or thinking or feeling in dealings with
the outside world (J) to help clarify which is the dominant
personality trait for each individual.

Thus the judging function (thinking or feeling) dominant
(J) becomes EST, ENT, ESFJ, ENFJ, INTJ, INFJ, ISTJ and
ISFJ. The perceiving function dominant (P) includes ENTP,

HOW TO MAKE BAD GUYS FINISH LAST
ENFP, ESTP, ESFP, ISTP, INTP, ISFP and INFP

ESTJ -- The Dominant Entrepreneur Personality

This extroverted type judges his environments through thinking, his dominant function; draws his conclusions from objective, external information. The external world is his reality and he demands that the rest of the world conform to his view of it. He interprets his environment through logic and careful organization. When a decision must be put on the table he readily supplies one. The ESTJ person readily grasps information, is apt to create new venues

ENTJ - Like the ESTJ, he judges his environments through thinking, but vision -- and a sense of possibilities -- enter the picture. His dominant judgment function is based upon grasping the meaning of facts and things and their unique associations.

An ENTJ and an ESTJ might find mutual understanding in offering opinions, but would violently disagree as to whether their opinions were based on fact or fiction. The ENTJ is a natural 'commandant' who insists on ruling by his particular vision. In organizations, he is the one who looks to the future and conceives new ventures. If the tertiary sensing function is not brought into play, formulations may be nothing than pure fantasy. He is able to balance his vision with relevant facts

Are you confused? So was I. My mind does not readily make the transition from the written word to abbreviations. Obviously the Briggsses are very comfortable developing these concepts. This portion of their narrative is included for those who excel at this admitedly deeper look at the concepts which govern entrepreneus and entrepreneurship.

FOR BELIEVERS

To those of us who believe in some kind of divine guidance, eternal purpose, and ideal of service to Deity and fellowmen, the following is dedicated. Non-believers are invited to read these accounts and come to their own conclusions.

For my wife and me, business has always been -- first and foremost -- a vehicle, a means to provide the financial flexibility to enable us to serve in any capacity to which we are called by His Servants. Our total combined *full-time* voluntary religious service spans 20 years, one-fifth of a century, with all but one year in foreign countries.

A former U.S. Congressman, who was my mentor in college, decried my decision to interrupt higher education to devote 34 months as a Mormon missionary in Argentina.

"What a loss," he said, shaking his head. "When you return, your classmates will have all the good jobs and you will be left behind."

As I write this, our net worth is several times that of all but possibly one of my former classmates. We have never suffered by putting God and His Son first.

Putting Him First - AWICO, INC.

Our kitchen cabinet manufacturing enterprise was progressing, in spite of pressure from a competitor. Asked to bid on a kitchen cabinets for a housing project, we were assured that the successful bidder would be awarded *several million dollars* in subsequent contracts.

A formal bid opening was scheduled for a Monday at 2:00 p.m. The previous weekend had been devoted to religious conferences with a visiting authority of our church. Monday morning the telephone rang with a call from the authority, "Today, I would like to visit church members in outlying areas."

I did not have to consider. A decision had been made many years earlier to do anything the Lord asked. The Sales Manager was shocked to hear that he was to attend the bid opening in my place. We discussed strategy:

1. Our competitor's custom was to prepare two sealed bids, one higher than the other.

2. The value of the contract was, at a maximum, $150,000.

3. The competitor would expect us to offer something less than that. We considered $149,000. But, their owner, Mr. Y, would assume that's what we would do, and bid $148,000. Therefore, we would bid $147,500.

4. At 10 or 15 minutes before the bid's scheduled opening, Mr. Y (who did not know our Sales Manager) would see that I was not there. Figuring that no bid would be tendered by our company, he would register the higher of his two bids.

5. At 5 minutes before the bid opening, the Sales Manager would register our sealed bid.

Visits to church members were well-received and rewarding. At 2:20 p.m., I telephoned the Sales Manager.

"Mr. Russell, you must have a friend 'up there'. We won the bid by $137. Since our bid was so close and you weren't here, our competitor was convinced we paid off their Vice President for Sales and fired him, on the spot!"

The "Promise".

Assigned to a three-year calling as volunteer Mission President for the Mormon Church in Uruguay and Paraguay, we decided that, in order to maintain our standard of living and support two children in college, we would have to dip into our assets for tens of thousands of dollars.

It came to me, almost as a direct message, that whatever we spent during our assignment would be reimbursed to us, and that upon our return home our Balance Sheet would be unchanged. I had no idea how this would happen.

Dorothy began to attend dealer auctions in Montevideo, Uruguay. She bid on 18-carat gold bracelets, chains, and gem-encrusted jewelry -- all at the $45 per ounce market price for gold. When we had her collection appraised in Florida, three years later, gold prices had soared. The total appraised amount -- less payments to the auctioneer -- fully replenished our Balance Sheet, according to His promise.

We believe that, when we are in truly in the service of God and our fellowmen, we are entitled to guidance in our financial affairs and, at the very least, forced to be creative.

Only one of our friends improved his financial position during our absence. Others suffered losses. I told one former associate that, had he gone with us, he'd still be wealthy!.

The reader, a Believer, will comprehend.

Replenishing

Over a decade ago, Dorothy was a real estate saleswoman, I was a management consultant. But I was spending nearly full-time to raise the local members's 30 percent share of a million dollar "stake center" (which our faithful members along the Space Coast of Florida contributed in less than 6 months).

"How much do you think we earned together, last year?" Dorothy asked.

"I don't know. How much?"

She mentioned an amount in high four figures. We had been living on interest from our principal!

Sufficiently motivated, I "hit the ground running" and our cash flow improved.

One night I dreamt of seeing a sign that said,

"Land Auction: Seaboard-something-or-other" (the lettering was not clear). In my dream I was told that we should get my friend, William Harrell, to go to the auction with us.

I told Dorothy of the dream. She said,

"Why, there's a billboard on Post Road advertising the Seaboard Loan Company Auction. You must have seen it."

But I had not been in that area for many months.

The auctioneer began to call for the bulk bid, a lump sum price for the entire 127 acres. We dropped out toward middle six figures. Then, as is the custom in such auctions, when the high bid is recorded, the total acreage was broken up into smaller parcels which were in turn put up for bid. This was done in the hope that the total combined bids for the individual parcels would bring more than the bulk bid. We were outbid on all but the last two parcels.

The next-to-last parcel of 27 acres came up. Someone made an opening bid. Dorothy bid 20 percent higher. The auctioneer became almost frantic trying to elicit a higher bid, without success. When he finally gavelled, "Sold!", so much time had elapsed that Dorothy wasn't sure it was still our bid.

The last parcel of 27 acres, identical to ours, went for enough to overtake the bulk bid. Three months later, our profit from the sale of the property -- triple our investment -- replenished our usual annual earnings.

In my mind, Providence had restored our missing incomes.

HOW TO BECOME A SUCCESSFUL ENTREPRENEUR

TRUTH

By Dr. Harry Hale Russell, LLD
(Grandfather) - 1921

Truth is truth, wher'er 'tis found,
Whether picked up from the ground,
From the dust and dirt and grime,
Or in polished sands of time.

Truth is truth, wher'er 'tis seen,
Though as diamonds it may gleam,
And sparkle and scintillate,
Or lie in unpolished state.

Truth is truth, wher'er 'tis heard,
Whether flying as a bird,
Far above the clouds,
Or in grim spectres it enshrouds.

Truth, my friend, comes before you,
Soft spreads its mantle o'er you,
and bids you to expect it.
Will you accept or reject it?

Do you close your eyes and ears,
Does it cause you bitter tears,
When it changes your emotions,
And reverses former notions?

Great discoveries of the ages,
Unnanounced by bards or sages,
Have verified Truth's position,
In spite of every opposition.

So this advice I give to you,
From whatever point of view,
When truth comes upon your vision,
Hold it not in derision.

For truth is truth in all ages,
Whether seen by fools or sages,
Prove all things, hold fast the good.
God would save you -- if He could.

HOW TO MAKE BAD GUYS FINISH LAST

HOW TO MAKE BAD GUYS FINISH LAST